HAL Amsterdam
From
6/14/10
to
6/28/10
WT Watts PhD

A Personal Journey to Positive Change:

Contentment and the Wizard

W. T. Watts, Ph.D.

e.mail   wtwattsphd@gmail.com

Order this book online at www.trafford.com
or email orders@trafford.com

Most Trafford titles are also available at major online book retailers.

Note for Librarians: A cataloguing record for this book is available from Library
and Archives Canada at www.collectionscanada.ca/amicus/index-e.html

Printed in Victoria, BC, Canada.

ISBN: 978-1-4269-1110-1 (sc)
ISBN: 978-1-4269-1121-7 (dj)
ISBN: 978-1-4269-1122-4 (e)

*Our mission is to efficiently provide the world's finest, most comprehensive book publishing
service, enabling every author to experience success. To find out how to publish your
book, your way, and have it available worldwide, visit us online at www.trafford.com*

Trafford rev. 9/10/2009

 www.trafford.com

North America & international
toll-free: 1 888 232 4444 (USA & Canada)
phone: 250 383 6864 ♦ fax: 812 355 4082

Dedication

To the Soevyn Family

Grandma (Loretta), Grandpa (Tom)

and Sis

With profound love and gratitude

Contents

Author Note

The author apologizes for any errors or omissions and has undertaken due diligence to acknowledge all sources. If he has omitted anyone, he apologizes and will, if informed, make corrections to any future editions.

Acknowledgments

I want to thank all of the spiritual teachers and messengers who have endeavored to make this world a better place through their espousal of inclusion, equality and unity. Most especially I would like to thank the following authors who have had the greatest influence on me and are most responsible for my current perspective as reflected in this work: Dr. Wayne Dyer, Ms. Marianne Williamson, Dr. Deepak Chopra, Lama Surya Das, and Ms. M. J. Ryan. Their dedication, insight and discourse have inspired me not only to broaden my viewpoint but to clarify that viewpoint through writing.

On a more personal level I must express the deepest gratitude to my wife Kathy and my son Dan who have always sustained me with unconditional love and endless enthusiasm. I thank John and Diana Lane for their support and editorial expertise. I owe much to Ms. Sara Steinweiss who was there from the beginning with both practical and creative suggestions. Additionally, I am so very appreciative of the patience, persistence and professionalism of Mrs. Ann Cosgrove who managed to decipher many of my notes and put them in a coherent order so that this work could proceed. My thanks to Mr. Mike Sabatini who in the final phase of this work came to my rescue and provided encouragement, insight and incentive, as well as clerical assistance. Without such help this would never have been completed.

Preface

I undertook the challenge of writing this book so that I may bring substance and understanding to my thirty year career specializing in psychotherapy and counseling. During this period, I have guided and commiserated with a variety of individuals, suffering from disparate disorders. In an assortment of settings and using variegated techniques including therapeutic mediations in public schools, phone counseling in San Francisco, crisis intervention in locked wards and both individual and family therapy in my office, I have related to and empathized with the pain, fear, confusion and irrationality of the afflicted.

My goal has been to decipher and define those qualities of mental health which are necessary to nurture and motivate a person to escape the grips of spiritual and psychological distress. I aspired to articulate a set of principles by establishing a core dogma which could be effective in maintaining mental wellness during both tranquility and turmoil.

As I advanced, I began to discern the insidious threats posed by the consumer culture. Furthermore, in a time of instant messaging, 24-hour news cycles and unpredictable shifts in world affairs, I wanted to determine the personal characteristics which generate either growth or regression as we are confronted with change. During this process I was spurred to recall both the stress and serenity of my youth and the traditions, testaments and truisms that served as guidance and refuge during personal turbulence.

The most vivid recollection was the first time I read the "Serenity Prayer." Written by Reinhold Niebuhr in 1939, it has always impressed me as the most succinct statement which summarizes the goals of mental health and moral development. It highlights three critical attitudes found in the book, acceptance (Chapter 6), courage (Chapter 12), and wisdom

(Chapter 11). With serenity as its objective, it humbly requests that God grant a bold transformation of perspective. I recite this prayer daily during quiet periods to instill calm and frequently during times of tumult.

I also recalled the times my grandmother taught me the "Our Father" and the peace and satisfaction that accompanied its invocation. It stresses forgiveness and acceptance among other virtues as essential to moral development and well-being (Chapter 6).

"The Sermon on the Mount" (Matthew 5:4-10) and a prayer attributed to Francis of Assisi (Chapter 13) likewise rendered comfort and composure as I grew and endured "the slings and arrows" of daily living.

Each chapter stresses at least one of the basic attributes (humility, gratitude, acceptance/ forgiveness, patience/trust) suggested here. Practicing these virtues as part of an overall life plan will result in a perspective dominated by love, wisdom and courage. With this mind-set, one can effectively confront and conquer the challenge of change in all its manifestations and levels of intensity.

The steps to such empowerment include: making choices with awareness and intent (Chapter 1), discovering who you were created to be (Chapter 2), and comprehending and actualizing genuine power (Chapter 3). By mastering such skills, one is in a more solid position to maximize life's opportunities (Chapter 9) while mitigating the culture's pitfalls (Chapter 8).

As I wrote, I noticed the uncanny similarities among these ideas which have been advocated by so many for so long, and the simple tale of a child from Kansas who is unpredictably plucked from the security of all she has known to be confronted with ultimate change; a new place, new friends, new ideas and a new life mission. The Wizard of Oz by L. Frank Baum (1900) is an allegory of self-discovery and empowerment wherein Dorothy, with the help of courage (Lion), wisdom (Scarecrow), and love

(Tin Man) learns that genuine power lies within and all else is illusion.

Overall, I think that I have expressed my previously unarticulated and clouded concepts about effective living. I now have a specific, documented ideology to guide me through my remaining years. I can commence life's journey with the certainty that I will be more aware, loving and forgiving as I encounter change and continue to evolve. I hope the same is true for the reader.

Namaste!

God Bless!

W.T. Watts, Ph.D.

Part I

Embracing Change

and

The Necessity of Chaos

"'Rest your brains and do not worry about the wall,'
replied the Woodman. 'When we have climbed over
it we shall know what is on the other side.'"

"'My name is Dorothy,' said the girl,
'and I am going to the Emerald City, to
ask the Great Oz to send me back to Kansas.'"
(The Wizard of Oz, 1900).

1

Chaos and Contentment

"Suddenly Uncle Henry stood up.

'There's a cyclone coming, Em,' he called to his wife. 'I'll go look after the stock,'

then he ran towards the sheds where the cows and the horses were kept.

Aunt Em dropped her work and came to the door. One glance told her of the danger close at hand.

'Quick, Dorothy!' she screamed. 'Run for the cellar!'"

"A strange thing then happened."

"The house whirled around two or three times and rose slowly through the air. Dorothy felt as if she was going up in a balloon."

". . . the great pressure of the wind on every side of the house raised it up higher and higher, until it was at the very top of the cyclone; and there it remained and was carried miles and miles away as easily as you could carry a feather."

". . . Dorothy sat quite still on the floor and waited to see what would happen."

(The Wizard of Oz, 1900).

Beginning the Journey

Change is life and it is certain to happen despite our feeble attempts to delay, deny, defer or discourage its occurrence in the hopes of preserving the status quo. Change presents an opportunity to learn and grow, as it assaults the person with unpleasant emotions such as anxiety, frustration and vulnerability. If we can be like Dorothy and stop worrying so that we wait calmly and see what the future brings as we execute a plan of action, we will empower ourselves to begin our journey of self-knowledge and contentment. With turmoil, chaos and change we have a chance to challenge false views about who we are and what we can achieve. We have an opportunity to recreate ourselves as we assess, react and adjust to new circumstance but we must have the courage to choose and move forward with intent and awareness.

As we respond to change, we create more choices and new skills on our path to fulfillment. If we contemplate change as meaningful, something to learn from rather than an inconvenience or a confirmation of our limitations and fecklessness, we can evolve and build self-esteem.

The fact that we have not achieved something does not mean we are unable to achieve it. Change presents the opportunity to prove this. We always have the power of choice and the choice is always between growth or stagnation, love or fear, acceptance or isolation. The central issue is to act on what we can control and offer to our higher power what we can't.

Dorothy was faced with ultimate turmoil. She was separated from her family and abruptly thrown into a strange land with strange inhabitants. Yet we never read that she bemoans her fate, pities herself or passively hides, hoping for rescue. Rather she assesses the situation with equanimity, actively seeks a solution and views the results objectively. She accepts each change that occurs without judgment then adapts and perseveres. Dorothy

5

is a prime example of a self-actualized person executing humility, gratitude, courage, trust/patience and acceptance in the face of change. She searches for solutions, listens to learn and focuses on achieving her goal to return home.

Chapter 1

The Challenge of Change

"There is no place like home." (The Wizard of Oz, 1900).

"You must be the change you wish to see in the world."
(Mahatma Gandhi, 1869-1918).

I. Statement of the Problem

"'. . . If I run I may fall down and break myself.'
'But could you not be mended?' asked the girl...
'Oh, yes; but one is never so pretty after being mended,' replied the
Princess.'" (The Wizard of Oz, 1900).

The most crucial question of our lives is who or what controls our fate or destiny. Are we the servant of instincts of which we may not be aware? Are we preprogrammed by some genetic code to behave in a certain way when presented with a particular external stimulus? Is every movement and reaction observed and evaluated by an omnipowerful, omnipresent, and omniscient entity who watches and tells us what to do? Do we have any influence, any choice, as to how we will progress through our lives? Are we the servant of random events or can we somehow become empowered and control our life path? These are some of the questions that must be pondered to attain contentment.

"The dramas of life are like weather patterns; inevitable changes within the course of nature" says Marianne Williamson (2004). "And every change is a challenge to remember what's true. Love is the only absolute reality, which never changes and never dies. Dwelling in that which does not change, while things around us are changing all the time, is one key to inner peace." The essential point is to face change, now. Embrace it and begin a new life.

Before we proceed, some key terms must be defined and clarified.

- **Change**- to make, become, or cause to be different.
- **Choice**- a selection, an alternate, a preference.
- **Will**- the mental faculty to deliberately choose a course of action; self-discipline; a desire, purpose or determination.
- **Intent**- an aim or purpose; having the attention sharply focused.
- **Intention**- the act of determining upon some action or result.
- **Awareness**- having knowledge or realization; conscious, informed, mindful; enlightenment, discernment.

Our goal is to become more aware and disciplined so that we choose the positive, life-affirming alternatives presented in our daily lives. In this way we will evolve and grow, fulfilling our destiny.

II. Nature of the Problem

"No matter how dreary and grey our homes are, we people of flesh and blood would rather live there than in any other country, be it ever so beautiful." (Dorothy to Scarecrow, The Wizard of Oz, 1900).

Power is behind our eyes rather than in front of them. We are the power which controls our life. Our thoughts and interpretation of events determine the response to change. Change is inevitable. You can never step into the same stream twice according to the adage. It is natural to resist change because it is scary. We prefer the certain, the routine. "The devil you know is better than the devil you don't." Yet if we are to lead a life of contentment, we must accept change, have the wisdom to learn from it and have the courage to embrace it. Without change there can be no growth. "Movement and change constantly renew the world." (Marcus Aurelius, 121 – 180AD). Face the fear and live your life. James Russell Lowell wrote: "Only the foolish and the dead never change their opinion."

As we learn about ourselves and our responses to change, we grow and improve our repertoire for coping with stress. We become slightly different people with each encounter. Our perspective begins to evolve, which, in turn, alters our behavior. Our emotions emulate behavior to bring about a slightly different self-image and world view.

A. <u>Self-determination</u>

"Whether you think you can or you can't, either way you will be right." (Henry Ford 1895).

Each person has the opportunity to determine and choose their belief system. We are all like blind men forming a circle around elephant. Each describing what he feels, although accurate in his perceptions, has a unique perspective. Once we accept this there is no need for defensiveness or anger. We can be ourselves and let others be themselves. We can teach and we can learn. We can forgive and be forgiven. We can love and be loved. The beliefs of others are just as valued as our own and are no threat, instead they present and opportunity to learn and expand. Learning and discovering who we *are* as opposed to who we were *taught to be* is a constant journey. It is a process, which pits prejudice (preconceived beliefs) against new experience. Here the ideal self ("should be") is confronted with the perceived self ("I am").   As we evolve and embrace humility, gratitude, acceptance and patience, the gap between the ideal and the real diminishes. The ideal merges with the real and we begin to treasure our true nature. Anxiety abates, confidence expands and we embrace the feeling of freedom.

Change is gradual. It is said that when the student is ready the teacher appears. Similarly, when the teacher is ready, the student appears. By realizing that each situation is an opportunity to transform, to learn about ourselves and to better understand our role in the greater scheme of things, we begin to achieve a different worldview and to peel away the myths that surround our sense of self. The path we are on is unique to us. From this path we learn about ourselves and our goals. Our path and our learning constantly evolve. As we try new things and experience different results, the view of ourselves is modified and this modification is always challenging and stressful. Life and growth are journeys not destinations.

Therefore, our primary objective is to define and appreciate our particular path. We must look inside and become free from the self-limiting thoughts generated in our past and reinforced as we developed. We have the potential to modify each moment, each day, and as we change ourselves so we change others. No one else can do what we were created to do. The final message, the final goal to achieve when following this path is to serve others. In serving we are served and in giving we receive. To honor another is to honor the self. So wave, smile, joke, and embrace life freely. Acceptance, humility and love are the keys to the kingdom.

B. <u>The importance of language, awareness and intent</u>

"The Universe is change; our life is what our thoughts make it."
(Marcus Aurelius 121-180 CE).

We must discover meaning, love and caring on our journey. Appreciate the talents you have and realize that only you can give these to another. Most of all give them freely without expectation of recompense. Practice virtue to become virtuous not for reward or recognition. Self-talk, self-examination and introspection are necessary components in this process. The reason language is so important is that the only way to make sense of what we experience is through internal dialogue.

Language both clarifies and limits our narrative. What we say to ourselves, about ourselves is crucial to self-esteem. Language is the tool the mind uses to help us master thoughts and feelings. Transforming the chaos of outside into some meaningful representation can be either positive or negative depending on self-talk. If we can learn to label emotions and the situations which cause those emotions in a more empirical, objective manner, we can come to an understanding as to how to react, thereby achieving a more realistic viewpoint about ourselves and our world. When this occurs we are better able to live a life of love, satisfaction, gratification and contentment.

Our beliefs are a filter from which we view the world and process new information. The longer we do not challenge these beliefs the stronger they become because they are consistently and constantly reinforced with each and every interaction. These false and biased beliefs become part of us, inseparable from our experience. We are conditioned so we simply accept them, without question, challenge or confrontation.

If we are brave enough to both define and dispute our belief system we immediately become empowered. We begin to see that few things are as we expect them to be. Ideally we begin to open up to new, more benign possibilities. Hopefully we start to see others as similar rather than different. The chasm between "me" and "them" becomes smaller to reveal an "us". We begin to include rather than exclude. Togetherness becomes a goal instead of separation, acceptance replaces conflict, and gratitude replaces resentment. We become humble because we realize that we are one essential but infinitely small part of a grand and beautiful plan. We develop more patience as we learn to trust in the beneficence of this plan and the wisdom of a higher power. Thus, these ideal dispositions propagate a social pragmatism that generates service, compassion and unselfishness which benefits everyone.

This progression fosters love, acceptance, patience, and trust as we proceed on the journey of evolution and self-discovery. The key point is that change emerges from within and as we alter our beliefs we begin to see the world differently. This internal reformation affects everyday experiences with our world. As Wayne Dyer (1998) said, "It's not that seeing is believing but rather that believing is seeing." As we transform our assumptions, behaviors and viewpoints, the assumptions, behaviors, and viewpoints of others change. Every moment of every day this choice presents itself, namely, am I going to fall into past belief patterns or am I going to move on and recreate my life. As psychologist William James (1842- 1910) wrote, "The greatest discovery of my generation is that a human being can change his life by changing his attitude of mind."

C. <u>Destructive delusion</u>

"'If this road goes in, it must come out,' said the Scarecrow, 'and as the Emerald City is at the other end of the road, we must go wherever it leads us.'" (<u>The Wizard of Oz</u>, 1900).

Problems are generated by external attachments. Desires, which are believed to be fulfilled from only the outside, will destroy. Emotions which are subject to volatile extraneous events will lead you to attempt to control the superficial rather than focusing on the internal voice. We must realize that perception is reality, our reality. As we think so shall we be. All choices and all changes begin with thought and in any circumstance we have the power to choose the interpretation of an external event and from that how we will respond. Each moment and each interaction provides these choices. Awareness in the moment and loving intent are the keys for appropriately evaluating and reacting to immediate circumstance.

For example, sadness can be the result of a feeling of emptiness, of not having enough. We will never have enough of what we do not need. Our culture of consumption teaches us that we are defective, deprived and deficient if we do not possess certain objects. We have to be aware of this influence and counter these messages with messages of our own. We can tap into the abundance around us every moment a thought of deprivation emerges by remembering that we are provided with everything we need.

From this perspective we begin to understand that problems invariably occur by looking outside (wealth, beauty, drugs, objects, relationships, etc.) to solve internal angst. Instead, we should soothe the soul by looking inward and taking command of thoughts, feelings, and behavior. Self-destructiveness is doing the same thing repeatedly but expecting a different result. When we pursue external resolutions we become trapped, myopic and rigid. We don't know where to turn and we feel helpless, empty and alone. We then seek more of what we don't need as we fall into addictions.

According to Einstein, the most important question in life is whether the universe is depriving, depleting, and defective or abundant, empowering, and sufficient. Is it partly cloudy or partly sunny? Each of us in every moment can choose the positive, the forgiving, the accepting, and as we do our life and self will unfold. You create your character as you adopt new attitudes with each action and interaction. If we view existence as meaningful and believe that we are unique with a singular opportunity to contribute to life and to others, we will find peace and serenity.

D. Basic principles for positive change

"Uncle Henry never laughed. He worked hard from morning till night and did not know what joy was." (The Wizard of Oz, 1900).

"Every change is a challenge to become who we really are." (Williamson, 2004).

Certain principles apply:
- Never let the striving for perfection destroy the good of what is.
- Never judge.
- Accept what is and make the most of it.
- Have humility by accepting your imperfections of the moment and embracing your small but vital role in God's plan.
- Be grateful for what you have and serve those who don't have your advantages.
- Be patient. God will do what is necessary in his time not yours.
- Realize that you are neither greater nor less than another.
- Do not allow the external to dominate and demoralize the internal.
- Walk with a bowed head but an unbent spirit. You are a miracle.
- Each moment is an opportunity to serve.
- Ultimately you need to challenge every belief that limits and negates you.

E. Thought and fear

"All we are is a result of what we have thought." (Buddha 563-483 BCE).

Fear should be of stasis, of standing still rather than of growth. Change will generate growth and growth is a process that must never end. Maturation teaches that we can control only our behavior and thoughts. Change is not necessarily dramatic. It does not have to come all at once. Rather each small act in each brief moment can result in a critical mass leading to contentment, love and serenity. Like a pebble tossed in a pond, change creates ripples which affect all objects in their path, moving more slowly and imperceptibly as they advance. Wayne Dyer writes in There is a Spiritual Solution to Every Problem: "What we need is a change in thinking to realize that a connection to a divine good, or spirit, or God, is what heals or eradicates our problems." (2001).

Discover and cherish your individuality. As you replace anger with compassion, hatred with acceptance, sadness with gratitude, arrogance with humility, conflict with patience, fear with courage, and separation with wisdom you will become more content and complete.

Every thought you have causes an emotional reaction. Therefore, you control the level of fear by controlling your perspective about change. Thoughts and judgments produce feelings which can be positive or negative. Thoughts are the end point of a process that includes filtering, judging and reconciling current events with past history, and preconceived assumptions. You are responsible for each choice in this progression. Emotions accompany thoughts because thoughts evoke emotions. Your truth and perspective are unique. It is fruitless to try to convince another of your reality. You can master your assumptions and the emotions they generate. As you think so you become.

III. Resisting the Inevitable or Spitting into the Wind

"All great changes are irksome to the human mind..."
(John Adams 1776).

You are not the same person and you do not inhabit the same world that you did when you began this sentence. In that brief period of time, babies were born, people died, and decisions were made by others that may affect your future. Your body has generated cells and other cells have died while you read that first sentence.

Despite its consistency and inevitability we fight change even on a personal level. We delude ourselves into believing that if we modify the outside, age will not affect the inside. We fatten and flatten dependent on the latest trend and the judgment of others that one area is deficient while another is deformed. The fact is that to live is to change. We have no control over the process only how we view it. The consequence of change is stress. It rips us from the comfort of routine and predictability. It creates vulnerability and uncertainty. It compels us to improvise as we scramble and stumble pursuing solutions to decrease the disquiet. We will not achieve contentment, wisdom, or love until we embrace change. But first there are natural and cultural impediments that must be identified, understood, and overcome.

A. Fear

"The mind itself is of itself, it can make a heaven of hell or a hell of heaven." (John Milton, Paradise Lost, 1667).

Fear is a very distressful experience (increasing heart beat, stomach tightness, increasing perspiration, limbs shake, etc.) brought about by an expectation of impending doom or threat. Additionally we appear vulnerable, helpless, and exposed. The cause of this agitation may not even be identified let alone articulated and discerned. All we know is that we feel alone and frightened and whatever will alleviate this anxiety is craved. Hence we develop denial, addictions, obsessions, and compulsions. What we imagine is far worse than what is. We project every conceivable negative outcome because the result of change by definition is unknown. So rather than distancing ourselves from our internal strife by objectively acknowledging what is happening (participant/observer) and planning our reaction, we run, avoid, and delay. "Not now," we cry, as we burrow into darkness and seclusion.

When we choose to think negatively we will feel negatively. The important realization is that we have a choice and that we are neither helpless nor at risk. However, this realization is the result of a process which is uncovered as you continue your journey to growth. Fear and all other obstacles to embracing change will diminish as you develop humility, gratitude, acceptance and patience. "Inside yourself or outside, you never have to change what you see only in the way you see it." (Thaddeus Golas).

B. Apathy and complacency

"'How can I get there?' asked Dorothy. 'You must walk. It is a long journey, through a country that is sometimes pleasant and sometimes dark and terrible.'" (The Wizard of Oz, 1900).

Frequently we avoid change because we are too lazy to muster the strength to look inward and make a decision to advance. It takes work to adapt and adjust in response to external transformations and turmoil. It is easier to deceive ourselves into thinking that all is well than to face the failure and frustration that is our own inner life. Suffering can be easier to tolerate than the anxiety regarding uncertainty. Additionally, suffering frequently comes with a bonus of sympathy and commiseration as others are eager to justify and corroborate their own opposition to transition.

If the pressures of modification persist (and change can be tenacious) our tendency is to seek an immediate external resolution rather than revise former behavioral patterns and problem solving strategies. In this way we squander an opportunity to expand and to increase efficiency and efficacy when confronting stress. Again, this strategy is vigorously reinforced by the culture and sometimes supported by our social network. Such influences prevent alternative solutions and hinder maturation.

C. History

"Even the pluckiest among us has but seldom the courage of what he really knows." (Friedrich Nietzche, 1882).

Unfortunately, we tend to remember failures far more vividly than successes and are hesitant to expose ourselves to further disappointment and distress. Instead of embracing change as a new challenge, we retreat to the comfort of the known where the main hope is to preserve the status quo. We deny, denigrate and disparage our aptitudes and fixate on failure to hide from success. We then convince ourselves that the challenge is too great and the world is too cruel for us to pursue excellence. Consciously or unconsciously our decision is final as we wallow in the muck of mediocrity. If you consider yourself a victim and begin to host a pity party, beware, because nothing will move forward unless you move it. All the excuses, regrets, and rationalizations only point to a determination to remain powerless. As we invoke the past to pardon the present we serve to make our jail smaller and stronger. We are imprisoned. We need to escape and face the facts. We have the only keys that unlock that jail.

D. A potpourri of impediments

"Behind them was the dark forest they had passed safely through, although they had suffered many discouragements; but before them was a lovely sunny country that seemed to beckon them on to the Emerald City." (The Wizard of Oz, 1900).

The forces which resist change are as numerous and varied as we are imaginative and self-destructive. The rationalization for avoidance is both creative and imposing. One way to identify our resistance to suggestions is the often used response "yes but."

What a marvel of mental manipulation and self-deception. With this simple response we simultaneously agree with the logic of the deliberation while immediately discounting it because some outside force is preventing us from doing what is necessary. Therefore, we remain immobile and powerless while in total agreement with the necessity of change.

Veronica Ray in her insightful book <u>Choosing Happiness</u> (1991) also writes of the numerous self-imposed obstacles to constructive change and the relevance of a positive perspective. "When we give up our desire for indisputable evidence of absolute truths, we can begin to accept some comforting, helpful, guiding ideas. Once we accept that there may always be some unanswered questions, we can choose our beliefs about being human based on whether they enhance our lives and the contributions we make to others." Among the impediments she mentions are denial, rationalization, blame, competition, and other personality traits and perspectives through which we judge ourselves as feeble, vulnerable and isolated. Such perspectives must be identified and defeated.

IV. Resolutions

"Things do not change, we do."
(Henry David Thoreau, 1817-1862).

As we go through the process of identifying injurious ideas and purposefully resisting them, both world and self-perspective evolve and we advance. This advance reinforces change and we mature in a positive cyclic reciprocity that is life.

A. <u>Embracing change</u>

"Each of us literally chooses, by his way of attending to things,
what sort of universe he shall appear to himself to inhabit."
(William James 1884-1910).

In order to cultivate such expansion, we must decide, intend and choose to accept the inevitable. We must surrender our wish to control the uncontrollable and trust in the plan of providence. In this way our feelings, thoughts and actions will be guided in a direction of genuine self-fulfillment. "Every circumstance, no matter how painful, is a gauntlet thrown down by the universe, challenging us to become who we are capable of being." (Zukav, 1999). Our task is to be aware of this challenge and to respond in a manner that propagates love and peace towards ourselves and others.

We must trust the goodness that is our center. Understand that we are spiritual beings inhabiting a physical body. Spirituality is our essence and it is spirituality that will enable us to conquer the corporeal limitations of birth. As this awareness becomes an intricate part of problem solving we will better identify and seize the opportunities to realize limitless potential.

We tend to be more frightened of power than dependence. Our destiny is not to be found in avoidance but rather in confrontation with our deepest, most intractable fears. If we are chronically sad, scared, angry, jealous or avoidant we must change our perspective and become beings who have the skills to resist negativity and embrace optimism. With negative thoughts come negative feelings, actions, and negative results as a destructive reciprocity dominates and determines our future. Therefore, we must train our minds to be facile, creative and optimistic when the unexpected intrudes in our plans. We must alter our problem solving approach and our attitude towards the unpredictable. When confronted with change we must reassess, reconsider, and replan.

B. <u>Seizing responsibility</u>

"…For I am tired of your city and long for the woods and country again. I am a wild beast, you know." (<u>The Wizard of Oz</u>, 1900).

"Be not afraid of growing slowly, be afraid of standing still."
(Chinese proverb, c. 1500).

When events and results do not proceed as planned our first reaction is to look outside ourselves for both cause and effect. If we are to achieve contentment we must first look inward for the root of a problem. Not only does this begin to empower us, but it also facilitates maturation and promotes problem-solving skills. We must cease the blaming and victimization that accompanies the abdication of personal responsibility.

Our response is our responsibility. How we frame a particular consequence determines how we evaluate ourselves as well as how we reorganize and renew our pursuit of another solution. This is critical to learning and empowerment. "We are one-hundred percent responsible for how we experience our experience." (Williamson, 2004). It is not an issue of inadequacy or superiority, it is a matter of choices which we make with the intent of acceptance and love or those which we make with a sense of victimization and defeat. In the first case we learn and proceed. In the latter case, we shut down and reinforce our stagnation and helplessness.

C. <u>Adjusting awareness, thoughts, and intent to change</u>

"She was surprised, as she walked along, to see how pretty the country was about her."

(<u>The Wizard of Oz</u>, 1900).

Happiness and contentment are decisions we make. If we change the feelings generated by events, we change both our perspective and our world. We then begin to approach life and its vicissitudes with equanimity, confidence, and love. It's never too late to begin this journey and to become who we were meant to be. We only fail when we do not respond to unplanned circumstances in a loving and self-affirming manner.

Through self-acceptance, trust, and patience we can actualize the intent to succeed. First we must discard past misconceptions of our worth and ability. Because we have not accomplished something does not mean we can't, we simply must adjust and re-strategize. Take control of your thoughts and surrender control of everything else. Choosing positive thoughts will produce positive results. "You can create your universe as you go along." (Winston Churchill, 1928).

D. Choosing a middle path (moderation)

"Complete abstinence is easier than perfect moderation."
(St. Augustine of Hippo, 411 CE).

Extremes are easier to pursue than equanimity. When presented with options, we are often tempted to choose the absolute because it is so final and definitive. In this way we put closure on the issue and cease further effort towards resolution. Instead, if we decide to consider further by using the stance of participant/observer, we more effectively resist the impulsive dismissal of responsibility and instead take measured steps toward a conclusion which we believe will do the most good for the most people.

The participant/observer perspective approaches all occasions with an awareness of the power choice brings and an intention to infuse life with love. It combines both an active and passive viewpoint of possibilities with control as the primary criterion. Once a plan is determined (by the participant/observer), the observer then assumes a more objective role of witness to the effects of that determination. Further alterations and deliberations follow as the individual assesses outcome as they relate to a goal.

In order to achieve such an ideal denouement to the decision making process, one must be prepared to:

1. Identify a situation that requires a choice.

2. Pause and determine options.

3. Reflect on short and long term goals.

4. Make a decision.

5. Strategize such that the effect you wish to eventuate will be realized in the most efficient and loving manner.

6. Act.

7. Evaluate results.

8. Reassess and restrategize as necessary.

9. Repeat Step 1.

E. **Reconstructing the past**

"The sun shone bright and the birds sang sweetly, and Dorothy did not feel nearly so bad as you might think a little girl would who had been suddenly whisked away from her own country and set down in the midst of a strange land." (The Wizard of Oz, 1900).

"Nothing changes more constantly than the past; for the past that influences our lives does not consist of what actually happened, but of what men believed happened." (Gerald White Johnson, 1943).

Presently, the crucial proposition to remember is that when faced with a choice, be aware of projections and evaluations which are based on your history. You should not discount these recollections, rather your assessment should include a healthy skepticism.

The essence of growth is acceptance of and moving from where you have no power, to confronting and challenging the situation in which you do. Our task is to embrace the novel with trust, patience, and courage. As we do, we redefine what can be controlled and what must be surrendered. We delineate and determine our areas of competence and with new resilience add to our talents. We become creative and confident. As this occurs we develop new memories and an evolved estimation of ourselves and our place in the world. If you think it, you can change it, so move forward free of past limitations. Imperfection is not inadequacy and inadequacy is not incompetence. The issue is to discover your unique talents and to use them at every appropriate encounter. Only in this way can we maximize our abilities and fulfill our destiny. As we accept change and have the courage to confront it, we will emerge from the experience stronger, satisfied, and steadfast.

V. Summary

"Two roads diverged in a wood, and I-
I took the one less traveled by,
and that has made all the difference." (Robert Frost, 1916).

"All is flux, nothing stays still." (Heraclitus, 543-480 BCE).

Change is unrelenting, non-discriminating and omnipresent. In order to empower ourselves and to achieve serenity we must understand that when confronted with a dominating force such as change we are only as strong as the choices we make. This is our power. We cannot control circumstances, challenges, or consequences but we can control our response and how we frame or evaluate both the initial situation and the outcome of our action. Each moment is the first moment of our new selves. The choice is responding with love and acceptance or fear and avoidance.

Our growth, fulfillment and contentment will depend on our answers to these questions. Are we going to surrender power to externals? Are we going to render ourselves helpless as we seek solutions by ceding control to others or are we going to manifest courage and take responsibility for our lives as we were created to do? Are we going to seize today's opportunities or will we delay, deny, and dodge? Are we aware of the moment and do we intend compassion? These are the questions which we must ask so that we may reinforce our humility, strengthen awareness and confront change with confidence.

As we develop the traits of humility, gratitude, acceptance and trust we will begin to respond to changes and challenges with confidence. We will start to believe our instincts and the benevolence of our destiny. We will increase service to society and decrease isolation. In short, we will behave with love, compassion, and kindness to ourselves and our community.

VI. For Further Consideration

"'Do you think,' he asked, 'if I go to the Emerald City with you, that Oz would give me some brains?'"
(Scarecrow to Dorothy, The Wizard of Oz, 1900).

1. You and your world are constantly changing and will continue to do so.

2. It is irrational and self-destructive to deny, delay, or avoid change.

3. We fear change because we distrust ourselves and our destiny.

4. We would rather be powerless than powerful.

5. Addictive behavior in all of its manifestations is both the cause and the result of avoiding change.

6. Our feelings are determined by our thoughts. If we think negatively we will feel pessimistic and if we think positively we will feel optimistic.

7. It takes energy and motivation to pilot change.

8. We tend to focus on our deficiencies and failures rather than our strengths and triumphs.

9. Many of us learned at an early age that we were deficient and disappointing.

10. We can teach ourselves to not only face but to embrace change.

11. Our power and our destiny lie in the choices we make.

12. Each moment we can choose to see change as an opportunity to learn and grow or an assault against which we are helpless.

13. We must learn to trust ourselves and the goodness that is our center.

14. When events do not transpire as planned we reflexively look outward for a solution or blame.

15. All power and resolutions lie within ourselves; when we look elsewhere we surrender self-control.

16. It is always important to remember that the choices we have are those which we make with an intent of love and acceptance or those which we make with an intent resulting from fear and victimization.

17. Happiness and contentment are decisions.

18. Always avoid extremes (the easy path) and choose reflection and a middle ground.

19. Acquiring the perspective of participant/observer will facilitate choosing and assessing the effects of that choice.

20. It is important to be aware of our prejudices and predilections when calculating circumstances before choosing.

21. The essence of growth is taking responsibility for our choices and moving on to the next event.

22. Our life goal is to fulfill our destiny by discovering unique strengths and using them to reinforce love and compassion at every opportunity.

Chapter 2

The Mythology of "Me": Breaking the Chains That Bind

"To be born again is to let the past go, and to look without condemnation upon the present . . ." (<u>A Course in Miracles</u>, 1996).

"When I remember that a short time ago I was up in a pole in a farmer's cornfield and that now I am the ruler of this beautiful City, I am quite satisfied with my lot." (The Wizard of Oz, 1900).

I. Statement of the Problem

"'What makes you a coward?' asked Dorothy . . ."

"'It's a mystery,' replied the Lion. 'I suppose I was born that way.'" (<u>The Wizard of Oz</u>, 1900).

The major obstacle to achieving fulfillment and contentment is our own belief system. This system encompasses self-evaluations and expectations, of yourself, your social circle and world. These expectations and beliefs have been inculcated into you both consciously and unconsciously by well-meaning authority and nurturing figures from your childhood. These personalities had their own stories and predilections which required them, albeit benignly, to impose upon your vulnerable psyche their beliefs and expectations about where you fit and would fit into their world. It was their duty to impart such doctrine. However, in some instances the child identified with the evil and minimized the good self.

Their beliefs stated who you were, who you were like, what was expected and how the world was and would treat you. Realize, that none of this was based upon any facts, rather this mutually accepted fantasy, set the stage for your future views about your potential and the limits to your potential.

As Don Miguel Ruiz writes (2004): "A parent creates an image of you dependent upon their story and their needs and they want you to fit into the image they create. If you are not consistent with that image the parent becomes hurt and threatened and then feels the need to control you, to tell you what to do and what not to do, to give you their opinions about how you should live your life." You then incorporate this into your self-concept and it can become a negative self-judgment because these false beliefs belie your true nature. In essence, you falsely assume that you are defective and deficient because you disappointed or fell short of expectations. In fact, you are as perfect as God made you.

Most of us are more aware of who we are not rather than who we are, which tends to be based on these early mandates. The results of such misconceptions can be low self-esteem and vulnerability to further distress. What we decide to achieve or attempt to achieve is strongly influenced by these largely unconscious ideas, which can lead to immobilization and disempowerment. Our task if we are to grow, is to become aware of these fallacies and influences, articulate them, challenge them and unmask our real nature. Each moment we must be aware of that which says:

1. We can't.

2. We're different, which is bad.

3. We must obey.

4. If we're not accepted we will perish.

A. <u>Summary of the problem</u>

A major impediment to growth is our ties to these myths of the past propagated by those who loved and cared for us. At once they are comfortably familiar yet restraining and disempowering. To grow we must face the fear of the unknown and embrace the power of life. We must trust in this power and view situations from a new perspective. Others will impose their beliefs on us with a threat of exclusion, disapproval or isolation if we do not conform and we are reluctant to resist because our tendency is to constantly seek the familiar especially as growth becomes challenging. Yet there is a solution and it is within your power to discover and implement it. As Fred Alan Wolf writes in <u>Dr. Quantum's Little Book of Big Ideas</u> (2005): "We create a past and at the same time, depending on the results of what we remember, we alter ourselves by redefining our expectations of the future."

II. Origin of the Problem

A. <u>Role of the unconscious</u>

"Reality is always much kinder than our thoughts about it."
(Surya Das, 2007).

All of us respond to stress and problems based on our beliefs and expectations. Such beliefs and expectations are the memory residues of past experiences and teachings. They are largely unconscious (happens without our awareness or intent) and yet have a significant impact on the choices we make and the direction our lives take. Freud's theory of the unconscious and the role it plays in our daily lives makes reference to similar phenomena.

B. Role of parents and authority figures

"The mind is a child. It believes what is told to it. Our lives become hell through self-created stories. But we each have the power to stop the abuse." (Wolf, 2005).

From birth we are told who we are and what behaviors and attitudes are or are not acceptable. Even if we don't understand the words, gestures and facial expressions of approval and disapproval expressed by caregivers teach us what is rewarded and what is punished, what is "good" and what is "bad." Eventually these mandates become more explicit, e.g., "you're just like your father, mother or crazy Uncle Frank." If we identify more with the negative themes than the positive, the seeds of future affliction will be sown.

Williamson (2004) concurs. She believes that a parent "creates an image of you dependent upon their story and their needs" and they want you to fit into this image they create. If you are not consistent with that image the parent can become hurt and threatened or fearful for your future. Ultimately, this fear festers sufficiently causing them to confront and control you. They "tell you what to do and what not to do." They try to force their beliefs on you especially regarding how you should live your life. Their misplaced apprehension becomes perceived as condemnation. Realistically or not, loving supervision becomes stifling denigration.

1. "Your beliefs are my beliefs"

"All suffering is optional." (Oliver, 2006).

The next step you reach as a young, impressionable child is to incorporate and assimilate these beliefs. However, although you begin to feel safe, you also begin to sense deep inside, a dissatisfaction, a belief that something is not right. You are losing integrity, i.e., you feel incomplete (not whole) and insincere. The unity that you were born with, the unity between mind, body and spirit is beginning to break apart. You begin to believe that you are not who you are supposed to be (according to your interpretation of their teachings) and you begin to believe that the essence, the soul of you is deficient and defective. You start to fear discovery because you sense the discrepancy between expectation and actuality.

2. Early tutelage

". . . information shapes our mental reality, our lives, our bodies and the material world we inhabit." (Fred Alan Wolf, The Source, 2007).

"I learned that if I roared very loudly every living thing was frightened and got out of my way."
(Lion, The Wizard of Oz, 1900).

We are also taught how we are expected to act in the world and re-act to the world based on who we are meant to be. "A real man or woman would…" "In order to succeed, be liked, not be taken advantage of etc. you must…" These rules of life are conveyed by adult modeling and early lectures. These powerful people instruct us as to what is funny or sad, what are compliments or condescension, and in general how to respond emotionally to various stimuli. They significantly influence the way we will interpret future interpersonal interactions.

We're also educated about our heritage and other family

myths, such as: "all the boys on your mother's side had big toes," or "liked to bark during dinner," "were possessed by various demons," "were great scholars or athletes" or "they just never got a break" etc. etc. etc. The sum total of this information presented to us when we have no alternative fund of knowledge or experience to refute it shapes the view of ourselves, others and the world, thereby shaping our fate. We begin to act on these maxims and then the world re-acts to us in a certain way setting up a cycle of expectations and self-fulfilling prophecies.

3. <u>Brainwashing and programming</u>

*"'But that isn't right. The King of Beasts shouldn't be a coward,'
said the Scarecrow.'" (<u>The Wizard of Oz</u>, 1900).*

The point is that from the time we make that cold, painful and unwilling exit from the womb, we are literally brainwashed as to who we are, how we should behave, and what we should expect from the world. The irony and tragedy is that these "truths" come from elders who were similarly brainwashed, as were their elders all the way down the line. Paradoxically, much of this is done with benign intent and is promulgated due to ignorance such as the adage "if it was good enough for me..." etc.

We are programmed before the "age of reason" and for many of us the "age of reason" never arrives because we unknowingly act upon and reinforce those primal beliefs every moment of every day. The pay-off is that we're happy because the world is predictable and our place in it is secure. We ignore, sometimes purposefully, that we are not reaching our potential, that we are discontent and that we are stuck. How can you achieve when you can't admit that you are stuck and powerless? Why change your ideas and beliefs when you're comfortable with this secure, established (albeit miserable) life that you've been taught you're supposed to have?

4. Growing out of ourselves

". . . no one who learns to know himself, remains just what he was before." (Thomas Mann, 1924).

As we grow, master language and enter the world, we begin to hear such "truths" from authority figures beyond our immediate family. We remain frightened and vulnerable. We persist in recognizing these significant "others" as omniscient, beneficent and powerful while we attempt to achieve more mature and independent functioning. These new people also have a personal story and they have determined what role you play in it. Similar to what happens with our parents, we tend to accept the imposed role out of fear and uncertainty as to who we really are. If they say it, it must be true. We also discover that to challenge this position creates anger, turmoil, and strife (because in essence we are challenging their very reality). Thus we learn to keep quiet, keep the peace and follow orders.

5. And the beat goes on

". . . but when you wear green spectacles, why of course everything you see looks green to you." (The Wizard of Oz, 1900).

This process can continue for most of our lives such that we choose companions, friends, and lovers who reinforce these beliefs. In effect, we allow them to tell us how to behave in order to preserve the status quo and our self-concept, as well as their self-concept and general viewpoint. The world becomes consistent, predictable and safe while remaining confining, disempowering and even painful.

Dr. Lorne Ladner (2004) in his book on compassion writes that we "are constantly creating and re-creating our own reality with each new experience or encounter because we filter our sensations from the external stimulus through the lens of the past." What you tend to project in any given situation depends on your past experiences. What's important to understand is that your own thoughts, emotional habits and actions in the past "are the primary factors in creating your current experience of the world." Every time you react to another person or thing, with a fixed set of thoughts and emotions, you are deepening your tendency to see a world based on those projections and their purpose is "to maintain a consistent self-image and world view." The repetitive nature of our responses reinforces a false sense of validity to the entire process of perception.

Ladner (2004) goes on to write that the "tragedy in all this is that it is a sham" based on the possibly well meaning but definitely self-serving needs of those who "raised and influenced you." You needed to be incorporated into their world view and self-concept. Consequently you were told who you were, including specific qualities and limitations.

It is not surprising that when we question these beliefs either to ourselves or to others we become extremely anxious and may be accused of being in an "identity crisis." The fact is that we are different to different people as we play out their story. Who we really are is yet to be discovered and determined, so as we begin to articulate and then question these beliefs we may be indeed creating a crisis but it is a crisis of opportunity not a crisis of danger.

Miguel Ruiz (2004) writes, "Before I was born...a whole society of story tellers was already here. Their story was ongoing and from their story I learned to create my own. The story tellers before us teach us how to be human. First they tell us who we are and who we should or shouldn't be. They teach us how to be a woman and how to be a man... They give us a name, an identity and they tell us the role that we are playing in their story." "I create the character 'Miguel,' and it's just an image based on what I agree to believe about myself. I then project this image to other people in society and as other people perceive that projection they modify it according to their own stories."

Dr. Wayne Dyer (1995) concurs: "The person you are today is primarily the result of interactions with the important figures in your growing up environment." He believes in seizing the moment and freeing yourself from the restrictions of your personal history. The idea is to embrace every day and see each new day as an opportunity to begin again, to create a new, more loving you, and to live the life that you were born to live.

6. The bondage created by a personal history

"Information offers us new meanings to old ideas and it affects the ways in which we conduct relationships with ourselves and others."
(Fred Alan Wolf, 2007).

"Having a personal history keeps us from the now." (Dyer, 1995). If you live your life as a product of your past you are manipulated by those around you. "When people know our personal histories they exert a certain amount of control over us. They expect us to be something that we have always been or that we have been taught to be. If we don't live up to their expectations they become disillusioned about us. Then we take on the guilt of disappointing those who have been such loyal sponsors of our lives."

Marianne Williamson (2004) also cautions about the human tendency to having the past dictate and mold the future. "Our view of the past shapes our present self-view and worldview. We carry this into the future by maintaining this bias and thereby contaminate the potential that the future offers. How many times do we say to ourselves 'I can't do that' and then proceed to fulfill that prophesy…"

G. Summary

"'I had the fun of watching them make my body and my arms and my legs; and when they fastened on my head, at last, I felt very proud, for I thought I was just as good as anyone."
(Scarecrow, The Wizard of Oz, 1900).

The views that bind come from well meaning caregivers who have had their own stories handed down to them. They have their opinions of who you are and the role you play in their lives. Much of their false beliefs and myths were imposed on us during the most vulnerable period of development and are largely unconscious. The only hint we have of their existence is the anxiety and general sense of malaise that comes when we make certain decisions, hold certain beliefs and pursue certain goals that are inconsistent with our true selves and the role in life we were created to play. We become depressed and passive as we focus on who and what we are not rather than understanding how perfectly us we are. We have to ultimately identify and challenge these desiccated, destructive beliefs of the past, if we are to grow and achieve contentment. We need to alter behavior as well as the view of ourselves, our social circle and the larger community of humankind. This can be done but we need awareness, intent and courage.

III. How We Maintain Our Own Cages:

Our Resistance To Growth and Health

"People will do anything, no matter how absurd, in order to avoid facing their own souls." (C.G. Jung, 1912).

How many self-statements and world-view statements do we make each day which we then desperately try to prove in order to maintain a consistent view of ourselves and our domain? How many of these statements are limiting, degrading and debilitating?

The self-concept is defined by psychologists as the sum total of ideas or statements that we use to describe and identify who we are. This can be contrasted with the ideal self which is who we aspire to be. The greater the difference between the self-concept and the ideal self, the lower our self-esteem, which is defined as how we judge and value ourselves, and how we view our effectiveness in navigating daily change. Conversely, the smaller the difference between who we think we are and who we think we should be, the greater our self-acceptance and the greater

37

our self-esteem. Therefore, if we are to improve our sense of contentment and well-being we must bring into better alignment how we judge ourselves and our ideal self. The problem is that our self-concept is largely a fabrication and construction from others and when we challenge this we are filled with dread and anxiety. If we dare to dismantle these precepts from the past, we must undertake the daunting task of making our own.

A. The terrible "shoulds"

"I cannot understand why you should wish to leave this beautiful country and go back to the dry, grey place you call Kansas."
(*The Wizard of Oz*, 1900).

In the early, more formative years, our teachers focus on who and what we "should" be based on their own values. Unfortunately, despite their arguably good intentions this frequently involves defining and emphasizing who and what we are not. These teachers are imposing upon us life altering rules and regulations with little allowance for deviation. They tell us in a subtle way that we must be consistent with their view of who we are and should be. If we fail in this endeavor we lose their love and respect. We become more vulnerable and isolated because we also lose their protection from change and distress. The real issue is that they are afraid if we don't live up to the expectations of their story, their reality and sense of self becomes bogus and unreliable. Tradition is threatened and their very essence and place in the world is challenged.

Such pressures incline us to conform and to ignore tendencies to do otherwise. We pretend to be what we are not in order to avoid punishment and gain acceptance. Obviously the messages imparted by these "teachers" is that I'm not the way I should be and it's not okay to be me. So we grow up, twisted and turned like a pretzel to become what we "should" be only to feel empty and dissatisfied when we achieve this illusive goal.

38

The perfect becomes the enemy of the good as we achieve more but feel less satisfied. We are left with a sense of emptiness, lack of fulfillment, self-deception and self-hatred. Ultimately, we strike out in aimless rebellion. We experiment, or we flee into an alternative reality or path, which may be equally destructive because we now meet other "teachers" who use us to fulfill and play a role in their story.

B. <u>Goals</u>

"'I have always liked you as you were,' said Dorothy simply.'"
(The Wizard of Oz, 1900).

None of this reflects who you are, rather it reflects who they are. Your tasks in order to grow are:

1. Identify and articulate these ideas.

2. Free yourself from them by behaving differently.

3. Evaluate the outcome and your response (participant/observer).

4. Build upon this to create a new essence and self-concept.

5. Focus on what you can do and the qualities you bring to a new situation.

The thoughts and emotions which you create with intent and awareness in the moment can change past views, determine what you experience in the present and how you'll feel in the future. Each moment has incredible potential to direct change and effect the results you desire.

Karl Jung (1933) wrote: "Just as we tend to assume that the world is as we see it, we naively suppose that people are as we imagine them to be…" "We go on naively projecting our own psychology onto our fellow human beings. In this way everyone creates for himself a series of more or less imaginary relationships based essentially on projection." Jung goes on to state that what we project is always part of ourselves for we could know nothing else. However, this part of ourselves is false and in fact we are limited in our own perspective to past events and the prejudices they bring. This prejudice is the natural result of the experiential process as we encounter the outside world and create new sensations through filters which are both painful to identify and difficult to discard.

C. <u>Summary</u>

"'If we walk far enough,' said Dorothy, 'we shall sometime come to some place, I am sure.'" (The Wizard of Oz, 1900).

We should begin to redefine ourselves by who we are as opposed to who we're not. We have to create a new self-concept by focusing on what we can do, not on our fear of failure. The primary issue which must be resolved is the conflict between our true nature (which we need to discover) and the dictates of those who influenced and "taught" us as we grew. This conflict can increase the discrepancy further between innate dispositions and the "ideal" self, leading to depression and low self-esteem. Until we can uncover, articulate and challenge the unconscious and pernicious belief system from the past, we will continue to assume that we are deprived, deficient, and defective and that we cannot change.

IV. Resolution

A. There is hope

"Undoing the past means forgiveness and re-creating the present."
(Fred Alan Wolf, 2007).

The key to resolving these issues is to realize and truly assimilate that whatever people tell you, about you, is their projection. It is their projection as to who you are and what role you play in their story. By its very nature it's totally distorted and irrelevant. The task is to discover yourself and create your own story thereby, becoming free from the self-imposed shackles of even the closest caregivers no matter how benign. As Ruiz (2004) concludes: "… you were born to write your own story." "If we don't like our story, it's because we don't like what we believe about the main character. There is only one way to change our story and that is by changing what we believe about ourselves."

B. Transforming our thinking

"I have always thought myself very big and terrible; yet such little things as flowers came near to killing me, and such small animals as mice have saved my life. How strange it all is!"
(Lion, The Wizard of Oz, 1900).

As we adopt different attitudes and as we change and evolve in thinking about ourselves, others and the outside world, we will create happiness and contentment. We will re-write history and our lives will unfold in ways we can't imagine. Additional challenges will appear and we will confront them with a regenerated confidence.

C. Central questions

Is the universe depriving, disabling and defective or abundant, empowering and perfect? Am I loveable and am I loved? These are the questions that we must answer if we are to achieve fulfillment and contentment. With each new situation, in every moment of every day we are given the opportunity not only to answer these questions but by behaving and reacting in a loving manner we can spread joy and further our own journey.

"Your personal history has attempted to convince you that you are one or several of the labels that you have been assigned." (Dyer, 1999). Our task is both to identify and articulate these labels as well as remove them from our identity. We must come to understand that who we are is defined by our behavior and reactions in the present. "I learned that you don't have to be saddled for life with the mental attitude you adopted in early childhood. All of us are free to change our minds, and as we change our minds, our experiences and our view of ourselves will also 'change.'" (Ryan, 2005).

D. More questions

According to Deepak Chopra (1997): "All of us were imprinted one of two ways; either the world is dangerous with moments of safety or the world is safe with moments of danger." Therefore, if we are to discover who we truly are, that is disseminators of love, acceptance, and inclusion we must focus on the latter view and eliminate the former from our identity and awareness. Is the world predominantly safe or dangerous? Determine the effects this response has on your comprehensive self and world views.

E. At each opportunity focus on growth and love

Dr. Wayne Dyer (2001) writes that the "greatest illusion is the one in which you look into your past and put your energy on what is there even if you find it reprehensible." We compound this blunder every day when we act and think in configurations that are consistent with early misapprehensions. Adamant assumptions have the benefit of maintaining both our beliefs and our station in life because nothing changes. When everything is routine and predictable we believe that we are exactly where we should be...right where we started. Therefore, unless you focus on growth and love each moment, you will stagnate, languish and decay physically, intellectually and emotionally.

F. Developing a healthy skepticism

"But I do not want people to call me a fool, and if my head stays stuffed with straw instead of with brains as yours is, how am I ever to know anything?" (Scarecrow, The Wizard of Oz, 1900).

Therefore, given what we have to overcome, these biased beliefs must be discovered, articulated and examined, intensely and objectively. You must begin to experiment with you. You are your own subject and what you learn and discover will help you connect with your genuine self and fulfill your destiny. With this knowledge you become empowered to change yourself, loved ones and those around you as well as your world view. On a cosmic level you now begin to change the world itself. You pick a flower and move a star.

The first step is to develop a healthy skepticism. It's not that seeing is believing but rather that believing is seeing (Dyer, 2001). Question your perceptions and question your thinking. Begin to develop the habit of thinking about your thinking.

You are now applying the scientific method to your life.

1. You become aware of self-beliefs and develop hypotheses to examine what results these beliefs bring about in your life.

2. You will evaluate these results and adjust beliefs and behavior accordingly.

3. After trying again you will re-evaluate these results and decide whether they confirm or negate your hypothesis.

4. You, with renewed awareness and intent, will then return to step 1 and begin again. You are now a genuine participant/observer.

As Ruiz writes in <u>Voice of Knowledge</u> (2004). "Now each of us has our own Tree of Knowledge, which is our personal belief system. The Tree of Knowledge is the structure of everything we believe." The biggest and most virulent problem with our inherent belief system is that it frequently tells us that we are incomplete, inadequate and inept. In fact we don't yet know who we are especially during a crisis. All we know is that we feel dissatisfaction with ourselves, our life in general and our relationships. Existential philosophers call this "angst" and it is extremely painful and unsettling. However, if you strive to view this unpleasantness as helpful, it can motivate change to start over and to free ourselves from the beliefs of others.

G. Coming home

"". . . I am thankful I am made of straw and cannot be easily damaged. There are worse things in the world than being a Scarecrow.'" (The Wizard of Oz, 1900).

Realize that you can never be other than who you are. Who you are is perfect in that you are perfectly you. Even perceived imperfection plays a role in growth and can engender love by helping develop empathy and compassion. Don't let your craving for perfection prevent you from embracing the real you. Remember, excellence does not require faultlessness. Embrace yourself and those around you. You are unique and that is good.

Your goal in life is to use your individuality and idiosyncrasies to interact with others in a positive way with love and service.

H. The role of humility

". . . I'm really a very good man, but I'm a very bad Wizard, I must admit." (The Wizard of Oz, 1900).

Another task which will help spur growth and mitigate stasis is learning to be humble. Learn that we need to learn. Accept and realize that it is a blessing to start over, to see ourselves and our world in a new way which we never dared to imagine. Know and believe that this opportunity comes with every experience, in every moment of every day. From humility springs all the other personality traits leading to success. It is the causation of love and acceptance both of self and others. With humility we can begin our journey to shed both the old and new pressures to be other than who we are. We begin to surrender and accept the principal that our destiny will be revealed to us each day and we will extract the lesson we are meant to learn with every new experience.

I. The myth of mistakes – the true journey to knowledge

"". . . I'm supposed to be a Great Wizard."
"And aren't you?" she asked.
"Not a bit of it, my dear; I'm just a common man.""
(The Wizard of Oz, 1900).

As we start our journey to growth we begin to realize that there is a plan and we play a small but necessary part in effecting that plan. This plan is perfect and there are no mistakes. What derails the plan are the lies and illusions created by our excessive devotion to the external, to the status quo and to fear of change.

Through humility we learn to trust in this plan. We learn

that our efforts at control were filled with disappointment and pain. We win this battle by surrendering and accepting what is. We surrender control over others by accepting them as they are and we understand that the more specific people distress us the more we can learn about ourselves. We take control of our lives by taking responsibility for our actions, thoughts and attitudes. We do this by being aware of the biases created by misconceptions of past memories and observing how these distortions influence each moment, event, action and activity every day.

J. Achieving integrity

"Be so true to thyself, as thou be not false to others."
(Francis Bacon, 1625).

Another skill we must learn on our journey is how to live with integrity. The origin of this word is from the Latin "integer" meaning whole or complete. When we rely on external possessions for validation we become parts, individual pieces of objects. For example, our car shows that we're macho, our house shows we're rich, our watch shows we are organized etc. Each thing represents a piece of what we think we should be. Not only are we incomplete but we rely on these outside things to define who we are inside. There is no integrity when we harbor such disparate delusions.

If we are to have integrity, if we are to become whole, we must relinquish the notion that only through possessions do we achieve status, gratification or satisfaction. Only then can we start to make life changing decisions based on who we are rather than what will please others. Our ideal self will be shaped by principles not possessions.

K. A new definition of success

"'For my part, I am content in knowing I am as brave as any beast that ever lived, if not braver,' said the Lion modestly.'"
(The Wizard of Oz, 1900).

To be successful we must change our perspective from the worship of and the submission to the external, to an acceptance, surrender and respect for the wisdom and guidance of the internal. We begin to acknowledge and bring to the forefront our own, inborn capability to live and prosper. We begin to revel in our ability to grow and mature without our own interference and desire to manage. As Pogo bravely proclaims in the cartoon: "We have met the enemy, and he is us." As neonates in the womb, we evolve according to a plan we neither control nor dictate. We just become. The same will be true now if we have faith, patience and trust.

In this manner we begin to re-write our story with love and acceptance for ourselves and our teachers. Part of the work is to decide, through objective observation, what to accept and what to reject. We begin to separate the wheat from the chaff, the loving from the fearful and acceptance from separation. We learn that we must love and embrace ourselves before we can learn to love and embrace others.

L. Tolerating different stories and different realities

"Our lives are made up of memories. Memories enable us to create rich stories, histories, excuses and explanations, all of which are put together from our reconstructed life scenes."
(Fred Alan Wolf, 2007).

As we re-write our story and as we develop acceptance of ourselves and others we no longer have to be defensive or feel threatened when someone else has a different version of an event or our role in the event. We accept our story as well as theirs.

The difference between the two interpretations need not pose a threat to either party. We are secure in our identity and in our role in life.

When we reach this point we understand that conflict is unnecessary. To be free is to be, to shed the myth of you, that perspective based on the needs of others. Once we achieve this transformation we can then reach a new level of awareness. We are content and confident with who we are and the vicissitudes of external turmoil cannot change our core, like the waves of a turbulent sea do not affect the deepest ocean. To enjoy the sense of self-acceptance that accompanies this state and to reach this degree of contentment is one of the goals for which we strive.

M. The "I" as a changeable concept

*"'Oz is a great Wizard, and can take on any form he wishes.'
'But who the real Oz is, when he is in his own form, no living person can tell.'" (The Wizard of Oz, 1900).*

Our goal of a contented life is possible because we realize our self-concept (the "I") is not a fixed, unchangeable idea. Rather it is continuously formed and reformed by our awareness and interpretation of daily experience. Once we act on this, we cease being who we remember and become who we are in that moment. These moments then become expanded and generalized to future situations thereby altering the past view of ourselves. We begin to perceive differently as we act and respond to our new sensibility, setting up a self-reinforcing cycle of perception, reaction, reassessment and re-creation. This new self-image is more compatible with our talents and innate predilections. We become that person who is consistent with our Creator's image and we shed the "you" of the past.

N. <u>Temptations to return to safe misconceptions</u>

"'But isn't everything here green?' asked Dorothy.
'No more than in any other city,' replied Oz . . .'"
<u>(The Wizard of Oz</u>, 1900).

As this growth takes place there will be sporadic but steady thoughts and urges to behave as we did in the past. As we change and grow, grow and change, those who influenced us may be threatened and attempt to pressure us to regress to old habits and behaviors. These people can be from the past or the present.

Do not allow any person to dictate who you are in the present any more than you allow those past caretakers to dictate your history. Ignore those boxes they want to put you in. Be free of both the good and bad opinions of others. It's neither your business nor your concern. Chart your own course, steer steadily, focus and achieve.

Enjoy the journey of self-discovery. It is a lifelong journey with no end. As you live to your full potential you are creating and recreating yourself and your world. Detach from outside influences. Be bold. Think and behave differently and note your changed thoughts and feelings. Note also the evolution of acquaintances as they respond to the new you. Accept that what is happening with others is beyond your control. What is unfolding before you is like watching a movie. You can evaluate it and you can view it but you cannot change it. Their script is already written, but yours is being reformulated and redesigned.

According to Dr. Wayne Dyer (1995), the realization that your true self is the "witness" behind the event (participant/observer) will bring you "a new dimension of creativity and bliss." You will discover yourself ever more authentically. You begin to realize that you can be greater than that which bothers you. Now you have the ability to detach from the present while being in the present. You detach and observe. You pause, fast forward, rewind or shut off the power as you review your experiences. You thereby affirm the capacity to chose and react to that choice in order to become a product of your own creation with each circumstance and each response. You become the hero of your own story which you write, edit and produce. You are now fully empowered and responsible.

O. There is a plan

"'That will be hard climb,' said the Scarecrow, 'but we must get over the hill, nevertheless.'" (The Wizard of Oz, 1900).

As you shed the past you will discover that each new situation does not occur by happenstance. Rather it is an opportunity to continue to redefine yourself and reinforce the new you. The power within is untested and even you don't know where it will lead. However, if you accept the present moment "as is," with loving trust and awareness, and your intent is to grow in love and acceptance, you will find your real self and the falsehoods of the past will fade away.

Each encounter will be an opportunity to test the new you and to continue your journey. As you reach a higher plane and become more spiritual you will experience a greater level of connectedness to all things and you will better understand your special place in the world.

As Dr. Wayne Dyer (2001) writes: "You will finally stop fighting and let go, even when you fail to understand why so many things transpire that are inconsistent with how you would orchestrate the universe."

P. Changing perspective

"I am tired of being such a humbug. If I should go out of this Palace my people would soon discover I am not a Wizard, and then they would be vexed with me for having deceived them. So I have to stay shut up in these rooms all day, and it gets tiresome."
(The Wizard of Oz, 1900).

When we develop an attitude, a way of behaving and a pattern of responding, we begin to develop a perspective unique and true to us, a consistent, integrated way of thinking, feeling and behaving. Even if we don't know it at first, our feelings and inclinations will eventually align. The more we behave in a certain way the more consistent our feelings become with that behavior and the more we transform our self-image to coincide with that behavior. First change behavior. Your attitudes and self-concept will follow.

As Williamson (1992) writes: "Love in your mind produces love in your life just as fear in your mind produces fear in your life." What you give to and expect of the world, you get. Love is heaven and fear is hell. Our growth depends upon shifting our thoughts and our experiences. We must evolve into who we were meant to be if we are to realize our potential and serve others. You are perfectly you as you accept love and face fear in order to grow. As we become aware of the "now" we must train ourselves to view life through lenses of love, acceptance, gratitude, humility, patience, courage, and wisdom. When we do this we will re-create ourselves in a more positive and productive way as the myths of the past gently fade from our memory. Zukav (1999) writes: "What you intend is what you become . . ." "Your experiences then reflect your own orientation and validate it." "Each decision requires that you choose which parts of yourself you want to cultivate and which parts you want to release."

V. Summary

The solution to overcoming past fallacies to achieve present and future goals lies with you. You must be:

1. aware of the problem and

2. intend to solve it.

This is done in each moment of every day as you decide how you will react to new situations. As we change our thinking, we change how we react and we reinforce our new identities. If we see the universe as loving and abundant and see ourselves as loveable and loved we infuse others with the same positive feelings which are then returned to us. As we grow, we integrate mind, body and spirit. Our thoughts, behavior and feelings become consistent. We are not afraid to include others and we are reluctant to exclude others from our life. We begin to feel a kinship with all and a serenity previously unknown. We become both humble before the power of life and proud that we are a significant part of the unfolding of the universe. We understand as we face the fear of growth that there are no mistakes only lessons to be learned and that there are no enemies only fellow travelers sharing a journey of discovery. Success ceases to become accumulation of power and possessions but rather feelings of contentment and unity.

VI. For Further Consideration

1. Myths about ourselves and our world significantly affect life decisions.

2. These myths are largely unconscious.

3. They were imposed on us during early development by mostly well meaning caretakers.

4. We are comfortable with them and we therefore resist changing or challenging them.

5. This meets with the approval of those who generated the myths.

6. These myths can be limiting and detrimental to achieving growth and contentment.

7. Through awareness and intent we can identify and challenge these myths.

8. The reward for doing so is the achievement of harmony among mind, body and spirit creating a sense of contentment not previously experienced.

Chapter 3

You're As Powerful As Your Thinking: Identifying and Neutralizing Self-Limiting Thoughts

"Day by day in every way, I get better and better."
(Charles Atlas, 1950's).

"So much is a man worth as he esteems himself."
Francois Rabelais (1494-1553).

Introduction

It is crucial to understand how we limit ourselves if we are to progress, mature and achieve contentment. Being aware of the past, our self-concept and our view of the world is part of this process and an essential part of the journey. Four of the most destructive self-statements are: (1) "It's not fair," (2) "It's their fault," (3) "I couldn't help it, (it just happened)," and (4) "If only..." We have to be constantly aware that even the slightest agreement with these will seriously impact on our journey to empowerment and contentment. Such statements while taking away our responsibility for unfortunate and unplanned results will erode our sense of self and sense of control. They will diminish self-esteem and lead to helplessness and depression. Be bold and be accountable. Take charge of your destiny. Admit your mistakes and find lessons in your errors. Only in this way will you grow.

I. Destructive Thoughts

"I haven't the courage to keep tramping forever, without getting anywhere at all." (Lion, The Wizard of Oz, 1900).

A. Origins of deficiencies, cognitive sabotage and self-defeat

We are trained from birth (or at least from the point at which we can first comprehend) to think too often in terms of deficiencies and weaknesses. We are taught by well meaning people what we lack and who we're not. We learn on a very basic level that we are weak, vulnerable and dependent on adults. We rely on their judgments and opinions and are therefore susceptible to their biased perspectives.

Everything you are is a result of your experiences and your interpretation and framing of these experiences. Your personality, your essence, is your memory and your memory is flawed in that it reflects the ideas and opinions of others. Awareness of this fact and attending to each moment of experience and each interaction with others will enable you to change destructive notions and re-write your history one moment at a time.

If you have the courage to let go of false images from the past you will begin to behave differently and thereby create a new persona which will be more consistent with your truth. It is important to keep in mind that every limit is a residue of previous teachings.

If we do not accept the limits and deficiencies pronounced on us by others we cannot be affected. But when we do not know how to challenge these falsehoods they become part of our belief system. We act on them and create a cycle of self-limitation. Such fabrications fester within, created by fear and ignorance. Progress and contentment depend upon viewing the world as basically benign, as we simultaneously maintain a more muted attitude of caution and query. Trusting in fate and ourselves, we must see the world as a place that is safe for experimentation, to learn and move forward. This is not to say that there is no evil. However, if we believe in ourselves, our destiny, and our higher power we can circumvent or conquer that which would harm us. The most powerful and insidious enemy is ourselves.

Our tendency to marinate in the past, to revisit old wounds and insults as excuses for current circumstances, must be overcome to achieve and utilize genuine competence. When we use the past to deny responsibility for the present, we wallow in the familiar and justify the status quo. We exonerate ourselves from the responsibility of solving present problems by believing and leading others to believe that we were given this hand, and that we were born defective, deficient or deprived, therefore we are powerless to change despite our best efforts. We reinforce impotence and victimhood at the expense of empowerment and achievement because we would rather remain dependent and immobile than change and mature.

B. Awareness

"So he painted my right eye, and as soon as it was finished I found myself looking at him and at everything around me with a great deal of curiosity, for this was my first glimpse of the world."
(Scarecrow, The Wizard of Oz, 1900).

The first step to growth and contentment is learning and awareness. We should understand how negative emotions and their consequent behaviors impede progress. We must also recognize how positive emotions are helpful. In each moment, for every event and interaction, it is essential to identify clearly our mental state and the circumstances impacting on us. Then we can more effectively choose a response based on its potential for happiness and success or misery and stagnation. In this way, each encounter refines our sense of responsibility and self-acceptance.

Happiness and contentment do not depend on what we have but rather how we view what we have. As adults, we are strongly programmed to reflexively think in ways that arouse both positive and negative emotions. As we become attentive to these biases we are able to focus attention on those mental states that reinforce the qualities of love, acceptance, gratitude, humility, patience, courage and wisdom. Such awareness and intent will lead to growth and gratification.

C. Summary

As M.J. Ryan (2005) states, "...I've come to understand that happiness is a feeling that arises as a result of the thoughts we choose to hold and actions we choose to take to increase these good thoughts. In this way we think our way to happiness."

The operant word is "choose" and with choice we set up a reciprocal interaction, a self-reinforcing cycle, starting with thought and intent, leading to action and then reinforcing that thought with further action accompanied by the positive emotions of happiness and contentment. For example: thought: "I like the way I'm exercising and feeling healthy." Action: more exercise and better nutrition→ reinforcing thought; "I'm doing what I can to feel healthy"→ reinforcing emotion: awareness of feeling good about self-discipline and empowerment.

II. Complacency

A. Emotions demystified

"... the little girl did not know of the wonderful power the Silver Shoes gave her." (The Wizard of Oz, 1900).

It is important to realize and understand that our emotions are responses (usually conditioned responses) to an external event. When an event occurs it changes our internal stability (homeostasis) causing a jump in adrenaline. We interpret this disruption in a manner that depends upon the current circumstances and our preconceived ideas. If we choose to define and view the world as friendly we will characterize random events in the same manner and therefore feel gratified. If we tend toward the paranoid or depressive end of the emotional spectrum, we will interpret exactly the same event which resulted in exactly the same physiological response as personally attacking or as confirming our view of ourselves as victims and we will feel poorly. The significance of this simple fact is astounding. It has the promise to be empowering if you realize that each and every moment presents an opportunity to change your life because biases determine which events you choose to notice and act upon. Awareness of this concept and the intent to be a positive force will put you on the right path. Bias and prejudice perpetuate themselves and once ingrained in our perspective are hard to diminish or extinguish.

B. Emotions and choice

"'I am terribly afraid of falling myself,' said the Cowardly Lion, 'but I suppose there is nothing to do but try it. So get on my back and we will make the attempt.'"
(Lion to Scarecrow, The Wizard of Oz, 1900).

Dr. Wayne Dyer (1999) writes: "Your emotions are physiological reactions to your thoughts." "Your emotions do not just happen to you; they are choices that you make." If you experience self-destructive emotions such as anger, envy, insecurity, depression, etc. consider your self-image to ascertain if these feelings are consistent with your world view. Challenge toxic feelings. Do you hold yourself in such low regard that painful emotions are part of your daily experience and are accepted by you as the norm? Just by being aware of your thinking you will deter and diminish self-destructive assessments. Toxic thought can be so habitual that it becomes as essential as the clothes we wear.

We should not shy away from painful feelings or threatening events nor should we revere, revile or ignore the moment because it arouses unpleasant emotions. Rather we should simply see the present without bias. Observe the event from a distance as a scientist studying a new specimen. As we free ourselves from the desire to judge and to fit each new experience into some old preconceived and preformed mold, we allow our transformation and growth to take place more easily. We begin to see others from a perspective of connectedness rather than separation. In this way we add to our power by feeling more complete and fulfilled. We become part of a greater whole.

C. Inclusion versus exclusion

"Of course the truck was a thousand times bigger than any of the mice who were to draw it; but when the mice were harnessed, they could push it quite easily." (The Wizard of Oz, 1900).

We now create a world view that is all inclusive. There are only shades of difference in a viewpoint of the same truth. In short, when confronted with a difficult situation, rather than immediately rejecting or reforming it, pause and let your awareness of the moment put the situation in a perspective which can provide learning and growth. Use the mantra: "This is as it should be." "What can I learn?" "What is God trying to tell me?"

"It is important to shift focus from what we are denying ourselves to what we are seeking..." "With this perspective, it's easier to make the 'right' decision because we are acting to give ourselves something rather than denying or withholding something from ourselves..." (Dalai Lama, 1998). We are therefore moving in a positive direction by embracing an action rather than rejecting it. We include rather than exclude.

Many scholars and spiritual teachers believe that whatever we target tends to show up in our life more frequently. So if you have a positive attitude, you will consistently attract positive responses and interactions.

It is a mystery why this happens but Ryan (2005) believes that "everything is around us all the time" and that we choose, mostly unconsciously, to notice certain things instead of others. We scan our environment and filter the numerous sensations which are available to us. Because it is impossible to attend to all the stimuli, we choose those that reinforce our attitude of the moment. Although such rash decisions produce instant gratification, in time they serve to prevent purposeful deliberation and undermine self-control. Therefore we must be aware, pause and think before we decide.

D. Summary

We create our own problems by choosing only certain events among many to validate the belief system we have about ourselves and our world. Each choice generates emotions and behavioral responses. When you accept any new situation as it is rather than viewing it as it 'should' be, you voluntarily give up control and responsibility for that which you have no power. You start to shift focus on what you can control and that determines your attitude and ultimate reaction to the new situation. Things simply are and your role is to respond with acceptance, love, and patience. However, destructive thoughts do arise. They are aberrations and should be challenged as you pursue your objective and affirm your spirit.

III. Resisting Limits
Origins of Self-Empowerment

"You see, Oz is a Great Wizard and can take on any form he wishes." (The Wizard of Oz, 1900).

A. Responsibility and happiness

We are born with power. Witness the "helpless" newborn in the room, who is the center of attention and with the slightest whimper has needs met immediately. As adults, we strive for the same instant gratification. We long for comparable control and command. We know we are in chains grasping for gratification but what we don't know is that we have the keys.

A major task in achieving contentment is to regain our power. It originates totally from within the individual. Actual capability cannot be taken away because it is internal. External status based on wealth, goods, social position etc. can always be commandeered. Authentic competence is spawned by being in harmony with yourself, your goals, as well as the events and people around you. The catalysts to attaining this aptitude are acceptance, patience and trust in your higher power. As you experience the sense of self-control and self-possession that genuine efficacy engenders, you will begin to understand that you are greater than the events in your life and that controlling the external is irrelevant to advancement and contentment. You are responsible for your happiness.

B. Controlling our thoughts

"A man is only as happy as he has a mind to be."
(Abraham Lincoln).

As M.J. Ryan (2005) writes, "we are free to choose what we will focus on to make us happy." If as Woody Allen states, the most important aspect of life is simply showing up, then we know that if we show up with the four essential attitudes (acceptance, gratitude, humility, and patience) our life and the lives of those we encounter will improve. This is our choice. This is our innate power. We must merely open our eyes to this truth and have the courage to try something new. We have the opportunity to re-invent ourselves by controlling how we see the world and our place in it, and God gives us this gift all day, every day. All problems, "...are illusions in that they are concocted by our minds..." (Dyer, 1999). However, it's intimidating to be in command without a direction or strategy.

C. <u>Developing strategies for success</u>

"...happiness is not determined by circumstances. Happiness is not what happens when everything goes the way you think it should go; happiness is what happens when you decide to be happy."
(Ryan, 2005).

Once your motivation is firm and you are aware of your bias and predilections, any destructive pattern of behavior can be changed and a productive pattern can take its place. Old habits have grown strong due to repetition and reinforcement. These are not an integral part of who we are. We are just now learning who we are and by substituting a productive act for a destructive one we will strengthen the positive and diminish the negative self. The keys are intent, awareness and attitude. If we begin to approach new situations with an intent to substitute a benevolent act for an abrasive act and we are alert to the moment, our attitude and circumstances will be transformed.

As we begin, every effort that we invest in changing gives momentum to the intent and reinforces the new, healthier and more harmonious pattern. Contentment lies in the ability to empower ourselves, overcome fear and allow change to happen.

We must face the aversion to creating a new personality and transforming our belief system.

In developing a strategy, sometimes it is best simply to begin and learn as you go rather than delaying by attempting to create the optimal plan to achieve the perfect result. Move forward, keep moving and do not allow doubt to surface or impede your progress. Stay focused on behaving in a loving, humble and courageous manner. The worst that can happen is that the result does not meet your expectations. Then you must extract a lesson and continue moving towards your goal.

D. Fear of critics

> *"'Am I really wonderful?' asked the Scarecrow.*
> *"'You are unusual,' replied Glinda."* (*The Wizard of Oz*, 1900).

Are you afraid that others may consider you foolish or that they may be offended by the new you? If so, obviously it is crucial that you summon the courage to ignore those who fear your success and who express it by either mocking you or threatening you with their anger and rejection. They are afraid of your growth because it challenges their world view and perhaps makes them doubt themselves, as well as their own success. Do not allow the false assumptions of others to limit your motivation. According to psychologist and scholar Abraham Maslow the highest functioning and most content individuals (those who are "self-actualized") were independent of both the good and bad opinions of others. Focus on achieving your goal with intensity and self-assurance and what others think will become irrelevant.

E. Role of the participant/observer

It is useful to take the perspective of participant/observer when facing the challenge of growth. Realizing that you are not responsible for the problems of others is a significant first step. The difficulty is to understand and accept the fact that you will never have the power to solve the dilemmas of another. You can advise, admonish, advocate, counsel and/or encourage but you can never cure, heal, repair or fix someone else. It is not your role in life and you must acquire the humility to believe this. To love does not mean "to fix," "change" or "control". To love is to accept, understand and allow. Loving is empowering another to be all they can not all you want (See Chapter 10).

You may ask: "How am I to serve if I can't save?" The answer is that you serve others by serving yourself. By attending to your own needs and treating yourself with love, you serve as a role model. You can share "experience, strength, and hope" but your problems are your responsibility and those of another are theirs. The more you apply this principle to your daily life and maintain the boundaries between you and another the better you will both be. You must learn to swim before you can save someone else from drowning.

Formulating boundaries is essential to developing the participant/observer perspective. As you encounter daily situations and respond differently from the past you will observe changes in the world around you. These changes may or may not be what you expect but they can always serve as lessons or guides to help modify your approach. Such a stance will confer a sense of self-control and self-creation. As you separate from the strife even as you witness it, you maintain the calm of a scientist performing an experiment while externally there may be conflict and tension. You understand that you are not the manager of the extraneous situation rather you accept the role of observer. Humility and trust are the keys to accomplishing this.

F. <u>Summary</u>

"But who the real Oz is, when he is in his own form, no living person can tell." (The Wizard of Oz 1900).

As participant/observer you will begin to appreciate how external events have meaning and lessons for your advancement.

Wayne Dyer (1999) writes that you will become a partner with fate and not its victim. There are no accidents or coincidences, only lessons and opportunities for improvement and self-realization. The important thing is to process the situation with love, acceptance, gratitude, humility and ultimately wisdom.

IV. Choosing Your Future

"Success depends more on how you develop your talents than on how many talents you have." (John Marks Templeton, 2006).

We now come to the question of your role in choosing those experiences on which you focus. How do you intend to shape your perspective? What is your goal in life? Do you wish to see good or evil, love or hate, kindness or cruelty? What instances and events in early life have biased your perspective? What does this bias say about you? And most importantly, is your perspective leading to growth and contentment or reinforcing complacency and deterioration?

We have to accept responsibility for both our choices and our feelings. Yes, our feelings are a choice. No one can make you feel a certain way (so forget about the excuse, "he/she made me cry etc.") or act a certain way. Your perspective is your own creation and it is a work in progress. Presently, you are acquiring the necessary tools to maximize this process. We must choose to learn from our mistakes and then move on. This is empowerment and empowerment promotes progress and serenity. It is a reciprocal relationship because as we develop, we assume more responsibility and as we empower ourselves we mature. The result of this interaction is gratification and serenity. Blame and excuses spawn victimization and dependency. As John Scarr (<u>The Secret</u>, 2006) says: "The future is not some place we are going to but one we are creating. The paths are not to be found but made and the activity of making them, changes both the maker and the destination."

We now know that in each and every moment our senses are being bombarded with data. Most of this is screened (frequently unconsciously) and we become aware of only a small portion. This awareness leads to an assessment, then a feeling and reaction. The resultant behavioral response is a choice we make and can be positive or negative; that is, it can lead to maturation and contentment, stasis and anxiety, or depression and aggression.

The important point is that the power is within to view and react to the event in a manner that will promote love or fear, inclusion or exclusion. Understanding that this process is subjective and that the power within is far stronger than the power lurking outside will help us take responsibility for ourselves and thus avoid blame, judgment and subsequently victimization.

To summarize, when we have an unpleasant sensation, we tend to focus (blame?) on the person or thing that was present at the time the feeling was generated (propinquity). We then process this information with all the baggage from our past (including the stories of others and their opinions of us). We filter and edit it, once again, such that our self-concept and world view remain intact and unchanged. The result is a rationalization, a.k.a., a lie, where we are neither true to ourselves nor to our experience. With acceptance, humility and love this filter (editor) weakens, thereby allowing us to challenge former fixed frames of reference. We are then more able to open our hearts and move on.

A. Personal power and responsibility

"When you choose the energy of your soul--when you choose to create with the intentions of love, forgiveness, humbleness and clarity you gain power. When you choose to create with anger, jealousy and fear...you lose power. You gain or lose power, therefore, according to the choices that you make." (Zukav, 1999).

Each time you intend, you choose to refocus and become aware of the present moment. You create an opportunity to learn and grow and to become more capable than the destructive outside forces reinforcing the status quo. The internal work of self acceptance, comprises the intention to respond to life's travails by cultivating gratitude, patience, courage, and humility. As you begin to project a different persona you will be viewed and responded to differently by the world. This is the participant/ observer experiment. These are the keys to free us from the jail of our past, and to empower us to explore the future.

We can be all that we dream if we intend to succeed and focus our minds on the positive, which ultimately is love. The power is here not there; it is in our souls, in the essence and uniqueness of who we are. "Through the power of intention your experiences reflect and validate your perspective." (Zukav, 1999).

In summary, we now know that the greatest tool for changing the world is the capacity to change our mind about the world. It's not that seeing is believing but rather it is believing that makes us see. (Dyer, 2001).

V. Impediments to Empowerment

". . . and the farther they went, the more dismal and lonesome the country became." (The Wizard of Oz, 1900).

A. Internal resistance to change

"People will do anything, no matter how absurd, in order to avoid facing their own souls."(Jung, 1933).

A. Desire

For Buddhists around the world, desire (as in the need for external gratification) is the true cause of any and all suffering. Natural desire in our society is fueled by a multi-trillion dollar consumption oriented economic system and culture that preys on vulnerability and dissatisfaction with the self. Citizens are taught that they need to be revised, cured, or improved. They learn to want to be someone else, to have something else, to be dissatisfied with what is and to generally view themselves as deficient, defective, and deprived. Therefore, the constant message is:

1. There is something wrong in your life.

2. You are powerless to correct it.

3. An outside object, idea, or person can and will help you, if you can only afford it.

Another pill, another car, another vacation, and/or another partner and all will be well. Unfortunately, once these treasures or "ego extensions" are attained, the feelings of emptiness and dissatisfaction remain but added to a sense foolishness. As frustration and desolation intensify, we again look outside to find fault, blame or another remedy. So now not only are we unhappy but also we are told that we are incompetent and that is why we're unhappy. We feel defeated and demoralized; incapable of ever being content. The cycle begins again and the quest for an outside "cure" is undertaken with even more passion and determination. The rat is firmly in the maze, frantically seeking the illusive cheese as cash registers ring up ever more sales.

B. Happiness as the main goal of life

No one seems to know when the main goal of life became happiness instead of loving and serving. Some historians believe it occurred during the Industrial Revolution when most workers' basic needs were met and they were confronted with the concept of free time. Once this void existed, the need to consume, fueled by advertising, incited greed, envy, and want. This created a desire in the average person never previously experienced. It was a flame which could not be extinguished. As Dr. Lorne Ladner says: "Desire is always idealistic." By its very nature desire venerates objects. It ignores every fault and obsessively wants only that object. "Desire draws us toward objects like sailors drawn toward the song of sirens." (Ladner, 2004).

C. Origin of desire

The question of where such intense desire for immediate gratification originates is often answered by Freudian psychoanalysts as the "womb". It is theorized that all of the neonate's needs were instantly met "in utero" and at birth the cessation of this immediate gratification was traumatic. Those emerging and evolving never really recover and spend their lives seeking to re-experience this "Garden of Eden". It is largely an unconscious pursuit and when thwarted, manifests itself through feelings of anger, anxiety, envy, greed, etc.

Unfortunately, we come to believe that the craving for basic sustenance provided by mom in the womb must now be provided by something or someone outside of the self. When we experience "need" or "want" panic ensues because on a child-self level we believe that if the need is not satisfied we will perish. Furthermore, we have the belief that all our needs can only be satisfied by outside forces. We, ourselves, feel powerless in mitigating this tension and frustration.

Thus desire and need give rise to the regressive fantasy that there is a "magic", "all encompassing" solution "out there". This "ideal" state promises an end to frustration, separation, isolation, loneliness and vulnerability. It seeks a merging with the outside to provide a continuous source of satisfaction.

The delusion that power and control reside "out there" causes us to lose ourselves in an external abyss, as we seek to feel forever strong, safe and satisfied. Unfortunately, we ultimately experience fragility, fear, and frustration. Yet we never seem to learn our lesson. All that we pursue is not elsewhere but inside ourselves. We have everything we need within reach but the delusion of powerlessness and fear of obligation blinds us to this obvious truth. Only we can be responsible for our fate.

In summary, desire annoys, frustrates and distracts. To be aware of what is true, one must only look inward. We must lose the impulse to search outside of ourselves for satisfaction, understanding and validity. Comprehending the nature and origins of need and want can help us in this quest. To be content is to be satisfied with who you are, what you are and what you have. This is authentic power and ultimate freedom. To be content is to be able to distinguish between needs and wants. It's to see the cup as always half full and to be grateful. It includes striving to become what your creator intended. Contentment is to be aware that life's mission is consequential and it is an unceasing quest for wisdom, love and compassion.

D. The insanity of repetition-compulsion

"I've been groaning for more than a year, and no one has ever heard me or come to help me." (Woodman, The Wizard of Oz, 1900).

There is another potent obstacle to change which also originates within. Freud called it "repetition–compulsion." This is a drive to do the same thing while magically expecting a different result. It is so strong that it over-rides the pleasure principle (the desire to feel good above all else). When a pattern of thought, feeling and/or behavior is customary and established in our response repertoire, the tendency is to repeat it despite the fact that it brings more suffering than satisfaction.

Many 12 step programs see this as a key characteristic of an addict and use it as a definition of insanity. While repetition-compulsion may be more an indication of self-destructiveness than insanity the point is the same. Our tendency as human beings is to resist change and growth. We prefer to remain in familiar settings which entrap, reduce and inhibit us. Rather than change, the inclination is to blame the situation on anything or anyone but ourselves reinforcing feelings of victimization and impotence.

To summarize, "the devil you know is better than the devil you don't" and the lure of the familiar is powerful. This tendency can be fatal as in the case of abused spouses remaining in the abusive situation. Therefore, we must fearlessly look at our current circumstances and confront any susceptibility to resist growth and embrace pain. We must get off the treadmill of repetitive, self-destructive thoughts, feelings and actions. We need to cultivate the courage to change and expand. Repetition-compulsion is the reason we witness so many talented people not fulfilling their potential and chronically stuck in painful, demeaning predicaments.

B. Practical strategies for success

"Far better it is to dare mighty things, to win glorious triumphs, even though checkered by failure, than to take rank with those poor spirits who neither enjoy much, nor suffer much, because they live in the gray twilight that knows not victory nor defeat."
(Theodore Roosevelt, 1899).

A. Self-talk

When you are aware of the moment, create an internal dialogue ("self-talk") which summarizes:

    A. The situation as you see it.

    B. Your interpretation of it.

    C. The feelings you are experiencing in the "now".

    D. Your strategy for a behavioral reaction. This can be extremely helpful in promoting the perspective of participant/observer as you analyze current circumstances objectively.

This strategy will better enable you to:

    A. pause

    B. clarify attendant emotions

    C. examine the provoking thought

    D. counter or reinforce this thought, depending on whether it expresses your new goals and identity

Try to understand the moment rather than judge yourself or your feelings. Do not censure yourself. Let all thoughts be internally articulated. Remember, you are not a bad person because you are feeling badly or (helpless, alone and/or damaged). These are only thoughts and feelings coming into your awareness based on external stimuli. They are not you nor do they define you. They are merely momentary intrusions which you will acknowledge, characterize and catalogue. After this you will then objectively evaluate the potential result of your actions and re-actions. Accept yourself, the situation and the people around you as opportunities to learn and grow. Seize the moment and remember that the best teacher is the person or situation which provokes the strongest negative feelings because such a reaction points to issues which you suppress.

Be calm and pause. Be aware of your breathing. Do not act irrationally or impulsively. For this process, to be successful it should begin with the attitudes of humility, acceptance, gratitude, and patience. You already have the humility to pause rather than dominate. You can accept the situation as you perceive it and you are appreciative for this awareness. Finally, you have the patience and trust that the predicament will be resolved. Courage and wisdom are the results of such self-knowledge and self-acceptance. Approaching a new situation in this manner and with these attitudes will lead you to a more peaceful, fulfilling life.

To summarize, words and internal dialogue are the tools we use to gain awareness and insight about ourselves, others and the world. In this way we frame thoughts and feelings as we plan our behavioral reaction. We are now taking the first step to wisdom because we are thinking about our thinking; then adjusting, observing and possibly re-adjusting. Our destiny lies in the words we use to articulate the universe, ourselves and our goals. Be aware of your self-talk and change your life. Herein resides much of your power. As Marianne Williamson writes in <u>Return to Love</u> (1992): "Thought is Cause; experience is Effect. If you don't like the effects in your life, you have to change the nature of your thinking."

B. <u>Focus on the positive</u>

You can either get what you want or what you don't want depending upon your focus and intent. This is why it is crucial to focus and intend the positive. Instead of stating your goals in negative terms such as "I don't want to be poor" or "I don't want to be angry." Intend and self-state, "I want all that life offers" or "I want to be kind and patient". As Wayne Dyer (1999) writes: "You cannot manifest prosperity by engaging in self-talk such as 'I hate being poor.'"

C. <u>Role of humility in optimism</u>

"'Only a mouse!' cried the little animal, indignantly. 'Why, I am Queen--the Queen of all the field mice!'"(<u>The Wizard of Oz</u> 1900).

Optimistic thinkers tend to see negative events as temporary and not due to something they did or for which they are responsible. "Pessimistic folks . . . tend to see negative events as permanent, pervasive, and their fault." (Ryan, 2005). It appears that pessimists need to perceive control where there is none in order to ward off feelings of vulnerability and incompetence. Such is the destructive complacence pessimism produces. In general, research suggests that some individuals would prefer to feel guilty and take responsibility for what they can't control rather than feel vulnerable and at the mercy of outside forces. They do not trust their higher power. They lack the humility and trust to allow events to unfold without their input.

To summarize: "Attitudes are the underpinnings of action...we can't change the outside world until and unless we transform our thinking, transform the way we imagine ourselves and our reality. The good news is that we really can decide to see the glass as half-full rather than half-empty and that decision will have profoundly positive effects not only on our happiness and that of those around us, but on the way our whole lives unfold." (Ryan, 2005).

D. The importance of self-love

People tend to believe that love is experienced only in a relationship. They assume: "If I am alone and have no significant other I am unloved and unlovable." Thus we learn to become dependent on other people to help us feel totally and permanently loved. This thinking deprives us of the power within, lowers our self-esteem, leads to depression and makes it extremely difficult to climb out of the hole which we dig for ourselves.

The first rule of hole digging is when you want to get out, stop digging. It is of vital importance if we are to mature and achieve fulfillment that we learn to develop a loving relationship with the most important person in the world – ourselves. The Self is the source of love and all related emotions, acceptance, gratitude, humility, patience, and courage. We must come into harmony with the Self before we can hope to achieve intimacy with another. If we value ourselves only by externals, whether they be possessions, power or praise, we will value others in the same superficial way. So focus and intend to love yourself without the bling, glitz or glamour. Appreciate all that you are and all that you have to offer the world. God makes no mistakes and you are exactly as you should be. The power of love begins with you.

Stop digging and begin seeing yourself as the perfect creation you can be. Stop the self-destructive, denigrating soliloquies and instead initiate self-affirming declarations about who you are and what you can do. Get out of the hole and into your spirit.

E. Service as a solution

"And if a lowly singer dries one tear,
Or soothes one humble human heart in peace
Be sure his homely verse, to God is dear..
And not one stanza has been sung in vain."
(Walter Malone, 1866-1915).

We are part of the magic of the universe and we become powerful by intending to make the world a better, more compassionate place. Individual power is achieved by serving others out of love and humility not for outside praise, recognition, or remuneration. Have the courage to offer what you uniquely possess and grow as you give. Practice service daily by doing random and anonymous acts of kindness to those you encounter. "The more you send out thoughts of: 'How may I serve,' rather than 'What's in it for me?' the more the universe will respond: 'How may I serve you?'" (Dyer, 1995).

VI. Summary

We have the power and the keys to contentment because we can transform our experiences, ourselves and those around us by changing our thoughts. By intending and choosing to see the positive in ourselves, others and the world everyone benefits. Changing thoughts, transforms behavior and attitudes which in turn alters the behavior and attitudes of those around us. Our future depends on many things but mostly on us. Each moment of each day our power is to be aware and intend to improve. This power will change experience. Problems and conflicts are simply reflections of ourselves. As we develop humility and self-acceptance this will become more obvious. You can give to the world only what you have cultivated and established. By being aware of and developing love, acceptance, gratitude and humility you will infuse the most powerful individual forces of the universe into all aspects of living. If you engender only attitudes of deficiency, deprivation or defectiveness that is what you will reap. Offer love and compassion and the world will respond in kind. You choose.

VII. For Further Consideration

1. We undermine ourselves. The fault is not in our fate but in us.

2. You created your current situation.

3. We are taught our limitations from birth.

4. We learn to focus on who we are not rather than who we are.

5. Everything you are is a result of your experiences and most importantly of your interpretation and framing of those experiences.

6. Our greatest fear is of change. Our greatest danger is the status quo.

7. There are no excuses for current tribulation.

8. Every moment gives you an opportunity to choose a different path but you must develop intention and awareness to improve decision making.

9. Happiness and contentment do not depend

so much on what we have and do but rather how we define what we have and do.

10. Emotions are simply physical excitement and stimulation which you then interpret based on past learning and current circumstances. You learn what is funny, sad, insulting, etc.

11. We should perceive feelings objectively, as simply more information from which to make a decision.

12. You must always focus on your goal rather than the impediments to that goal.

13. Once your motivation is firm and you are aware of biases and predilections, any destructive pattern of behavior can be changed and a productive pattern can take its place.

14. A useful perspective as you face change is that of a "participant-observer." In this way you view life as a series of experiments (trial and error) from which you continually learn and grow.

15. You are not responsible for, nor can you solve or control the problems of another.

16. The greatest tool for controlling our future is to change.

17. The consumer culture teaches us that we are deprived, deficient, or disabled and the solution to this condition lies outside of ourselves.

18. Due to fear we tend to repeat the same mistakes, attempt the same solutions, and feel dismayed when nothing changes.

19. Self-acceptance is the simple but elusive goal that will result in contentment.

20. The first step in all growth is to assume an aspect of humility. There is much to be humble and grateful about.

21. Attitudes such as humility, gratitude, patience and acceptance are the underpinnings of contentment and serenity.

22. Service to others will result in pure satisfaction, happiness, and contentment.

23. Distance yourself from both the criticism and praise of others.

24. Remember that you can always pause and stop the momentum by breathing slowly and re-connecting with your essence.

25. Be aware of your spiritual core and unceasingly intend love and compassion.

Part II

Building a Foundation:

The Basic Virtues

"I have always thought myself very big and terrible; yet such little things as flowers came near to killing me and such small animals as mice have saved my life. How strange it all is!"
(Lion, The Wizard of Oz, 1900).

Developing Honor and Integrity

Throughout the novel, Dorothy and her companions exhibit the basic virtues of humility, gratitude, trust, patience, acceptance and forgiveness. In fact, these virtues are so infused in their characters and behavior that rarely is there a scene where at least one is not manifested. If we are to understand our purpose in life, fulfill our potential and become who we were created to be, we must behave in a manner which is conducive to attracting others to our cause and creating a perspective where we view the world as our classroom. The most important objective is to cultivate and assimilate those basic virtues.

As the Cowardly Lion is quoted: "How strange it all is!" We need to begin with humility, from which all the other traits spring. Basically, humility is the belief that we are neither more nor less than others but rather one significant part of a miraculous whole. From this is generated gratitude for all the gifts we have and trust that God's grand plan is benevolent. We then progress to patience that all things will happen in God's time, not ours. Now we are ready to accept all that is in our life as all that we need and we are prepared to forgive ourselves and others for any shortcomings.

These traits have been recommended throughout the ages by sages and scribes, spiritualists and savants as dispositions which promote love and lead to contentment. As we mature they are integrated into our thoughts and behaviors so that we construct a world view dominated by love and wisdom. This is our goal.

Chapter 4

The Power of Humility

"Blessed are the meek for they shall inherit the earth."
(Matthew 5:4 – 10).

I. Definition

"I am Dorothy, the Small and Meek. I have come to you for help." (The Wizard of Oz, 1900).

A. Origins

Humility is truth and it is a truth that focuses us and creates a specific perspective, from which we may view all experiences. The origin of the word can be found in the Latin "humilis" for "low" or "lowly," which in turn comes from "humus" or "ground." To be a "grounded" person is to be steadfast in one's beliefs, as well as, solid and reliable. One must have "grounds" and facts based on precedent to bring forward a legal proceeding. The ground is, "the solid surface of the earth" according to Webster's New World Dictionary and Thesaurus. Furthermore, ground is defined as a "basis; a foundation", "a valid reason or motive" as well as, "to instruct on the first principles." At the same time "ground-less" is "without reason or cause."

Therefore, while its origins imply something negative ("low or lowly"), humility also implies something positive namely, being "grounded" or "solid." As a working definition, humility leads you to acknowledge what you can't control. This, in turn, gives you greater power over what you can control because it intensifies your awareness and focus. Consequently your self-esteem also increases because you begin to experience true power and efficacy. As physicist Gary Zukav (1999) states in The Seat of the Soul: "An authentically empowered person is humble."

To be humble is to accept yourself and to resist the temptation to either embellish or diminish your importance. It is to try your best, yet accept failure with the same gratitude that you accept success. As humble persons, we begin to view failure (neither getting what we want, nor events going as planned) as a lesson and success as a message. We concede what we can't control and we surrender our will, trusting that all will work out as "it was meant to."

Humility's opposite, pride, is one of the primary "deadly" sins and we all know that pride precedes the fall. Pride, according to Webster is, "an unduly high opinion of oneself, associated with arrogance, conceit and pretense." The Old English spelling was "pryde" meaning excessive self-esteem. (The Oxford Dictionary of Word Histories, 2002).

B. **Humility and passivity**

"'Why should I do this for you?' asked Oz.
'Because you are strong and I am weak; because you are a Great
Wizard and I am only a helpless little girl.'"
(The Wizard of Oz, 1900).

To have humility is not to be humiliated or passive rather it is to cherish yourself and all the life around you. To live effectively one needs to understand limitations, to have gratitude for help, to listen, but not necessarily agree, with other opinions. To be humble is to say "Thank God I am me" and that He has given me the courage to discover myself, to confront my fears and to cherish and nurture family and friends. To be humble is to be virtuous anonymously; to do kind, loving acts unconditionally and randomly without boasting or seeking praise. To be humble, therefore, is to be strong and powerful not weak or passive. It is to be empowered, because your self-esteem depends upon self-judgment and self-control, not the judgment of others. You are worthy of love and respect simply because you exist. You are neither more nor less. You are part of a perfect plan to which you contribute significantly. You realize that you have everything you need and you can never get enough of what you don't need.

To realize and understand how little we actually control will initially cause feelings of fear and vulnerability. Yet with trust in a plan greater than ourselves we may surpass this hurdle and become genuinely humble. This realization is an active, decision making process not a passive, impotent cry for help. Surrender and capitulation are different. Surrender is an active, tactical decision to move ahead by ceding victory in a battle that is winless. Capitulation is a passive act of giving up both control over your welfare and control over decision making. One decision which we will always control is how we view events and how we choose to act on that viewpoint. Every situation we encounter is an opportunity to define ourselves and to mature. Being humble does not cede such control.

C. **Humility and growth**

"I believe that the first test of a really great man is his humility."
(John Ruskin, 1850).

Humility is the strength to be vulnerable, to trust and have the patience to understand that whatever situation we face is there for a purpose. That purpose is to teach us about ourselves and how to fulfill our destiny. To grow is to develop and practice the traits expressed here while moving in a direction towards the greater good. Growth is appreciating that we have a responsibility to change the world using our unique talents in a way that reflects love, acceptance and inclusion.

D. <u>Summary</u>

Humility is a positive and desirable trait. It is something we need to "ground" us and to form a basis and foundation for a knowledge of ourselves and the world. It sows the fertile ground from which gratitude, acceptance and patience grow. It actually enhances self-esteem because it enables us to see and accept who we are. It empowers us to realize that we are unique and that we have a special, albeit small, part in the larger scheme of the universe. We have a purpose and we are blessed. Humility gives us the strength to be ourselves and to discover our true nature. It encourages us to strip away the myths of the past. Humility subordinates the ego/child-self which says we are dominant and our needs override anything else.

II. <u>Humility In Daily Life</u>

"All streams flow to the ocean because it is lower than they are. Humility gives it its power." (Lao-Tzu, 6th century B.C.E.).

A. <u>The true nature of humility</u>

"Humility is the most difficult of all virtues to achieve; nothing dies harder thanthe desire to think well of oneself." (T.S. Eliot, 1922).

What is the true nature of humility? Humility is simply an acknowledgement of who you are, that you are an instrument of a higher power. As John Ruskin (1819 – 1900) wrote; "really great men have a curious feeling that their greatness is not of them, but through them. And they see something divine in every other man. . ."

Humility is understanding and embracing the idea that you have a purpose in life, which is revealed to you gradually. All good comes to you from this center. You don't create this, you accept it. This is your source and the source of every living thing on the planet. As Marianne Williamson (2002) writes: "And as we gain, through experience, more and more faith in that basic goodness (of the Universe and God), we learn to give up our efforts to control and instead to deeply trust." If we accept this simple but frightening truth, (that we control little and that we must surrender our arrogance to a higher power) we can become part of the creation of a benevolent universe. Our role is to listen to our hearts and hear our source. We must eliminate the noise of the ego/child self. We must eliminate the idea of "me-ness" for the idea of "one-ness" and develop the courage to fulfill our fate. As we do this, our road will become more defined and our significance will be better understood. Ultimately, we will identify the skills which must be displayed and the manner in which we present them so that love and compassion fills our lives and the lives of those we encounter. This is our destiny and the road to contentment.

B. <u>Humility and relationships</u>

"I am only a Scarecrow, stuffed with straw. Therefore I have no brains, and I come to you praying that you will put brains in my head instead of straw, so that I may become as much a man as any other in your dominions." (<u>The Wizard of Oz</u>, 1900).

In order to achieve the goals of gratification and contentment we must first make a major shift in our thinking. We must free ourselves from the ego/child self thinking of "I," "me," and "mine" and adopt a life perspective of "we," "us," and "ours." Humility is the catalyst of this process and relationships are the training ground.

A major tension in all relationships reflects this struggle. This tension is created by the need for intimacy and affection (so that we feel protected and accepted by another) and the simultaneous and conflictual need to be autonomous and self-sufficient, free of any encumbrances. These contradictory urges create havoc as we try to bond with another. This is true from the most casual to the most intimate relationships. In all our interactions with others, we judge and create the "I," "we," "us," and "them"; constantly shifting boundaries and determining the appropriate level of intimacy to use in each and every interaction.

Out of mutual respect many Eastern cultures acknowledge the other, with a bow when they first meet. Some Asian cultures, put their hands together, fingers pointing upward, bow and say, "Namaste". Loosely translated this means: "I honor the place where you and I are one." If we begin with the perspective of "namaste," we create a predisposition towards humility and equality. We take the first step towards living in a contented, peaceful manner, where we don't attempt to dominate or control the other. We are not seeking power or superiority, we are not looking to exclude, rather we are searching for commonality, oneness and equality. Herein lies peace. What we put out to the world comes back to us. Love for love, hate for hate. Will we choose inclusion or isolation, acceptance or rejection? It is up to us and we can choose in every moment with each relationship to live a contented life.

Once we understand this concept and initiate all interactions from a center of humility, we begin to expand beyond the child-self ("me-ness"). In this way, we more effectively utilize all the recommended traits (gratitude, acceptance, patience, love, wisdom, acceptance, and courage) in areas of inner and outer awareness. Consequently, we experience and generate love and wisdom, while living peacefully and compassionately.

C. Humility and service

"The way to be happy is to make others so."

(Robert Ingersoll, 1875).

Welcome to responsible living, loving and giving. You begin to discover and understand that you are perfectly you and that you have an opportunity to present to others a person of substance, consequence, and confidence. There is no greater liberation and no greater task than to help and serve others while expressing your beliefs and being who you are with no ego, pretense or prevarication. Service to others is the ultimate expression of humility. As Dr. Lorne Ladner (2004) writes: "The greatest act of humility is serving others and this is the basis of individual growth and the foundation of love. We should never serve others for what we can get rather always serve for what we can give. If we intend love, we will receive love."

Lama Surya Das (2007) writes that we: "need each other to become enlightened, because the development of genuine wisdom depends on developing warmhearted love and compassion. All the happiness and virtue in this world come from selflessness and generosity, all the sorrow from egotism, selfishness, and greed. As the Dalai Lama (1998) has said, "If you want to be wisely selfish, care for others."

D. Summary

Humility is the center of all that we wish to become. It is the seed that spawns gratitude, patience/trust, love, wisdom, acceptance and courage. Each trait is necessary to achieve contentment and they work together to create a self-fulfilled life. Our focus on humility is the first step of participation in an eternal dance of joy, wonder, and love.

To embrace this message is to understand the meaning of life as it has been passed down from Eastern and Western scribes, philosophers, and "holy men". To understand this is to know your place in life, to act on what you control and to relinquish the rest. To be humble is to be grateful and satisfied, to accept, to trust, and to cherish. It is to be strong and patient. It is to reflect upon the "Life Force", the essential force of the universe. It is to live the *Serenity Prayer*, which for many is the definition of mental health, contentment and gratification.

III. Humility's Role In Achieving Growth and Contentment

"Whatever good you have is all from God, whatever evil is all from yourself." (The Holy Koran).

A. The necessity of achieving humility

"Rather to bow than break is profitable;
Humility is a thing commendable."
(William Cowper, 1731-1800).

If we are to accomplish our preeminent purpose, the first and foremost characteristic which must be defined and developed is humility. From this radiate gratitude and patience/trust, which lead to acceptance, love, wisdom, and courage. All of these contribute to a life of serenity and satisfaction. As we begin to understand the virtue of humility, we begin to develop the traits necessary for such a life.

In order to accomplish this, we must first know ourselves. We must fearlessly scrutinize ourselves to determine the essence of our individuality. We should make a list of our strengths and weaknesses and test and validate this list with observations based on thoughts, feelings, and behaviors as we go through daily routines. We then become participant/observers in our lives and we are better able to assess all of our attributes. We become scientists of the self. A daily journal can be most helpful in this endeavor.

With such effort and intent, we will indeed be on the path to self-knowledge. Unknown dimensions of the self will be discovered and thereby the spurious definitions of who we are will be dispelled. We are re-creating and re-defining ourselves in every moment. We become empowered and are no longer at the mercy of self-destructive beliefs or perspectives.

B. <u>Rediscovering and recreating ourselves</u>

"Aren't you ashamed to be concerned so much about making all the money you can and advancing your reputation and prestige, while for truth and wisdom and the improvement of your souls you have no thought or care?" (Socrates, 5th Century BCE).

If we are to fulfill our destiny we must see beyond ourselves and become free from the influence of the external pressures that prevent us from experiencing truth. As such, we need to re-examine thoughts and beliefs, and all the lessons of our youth concerning the world and ourselves.

We have to re-discover who we are and who we are meant to be. We must create and be re-created by our role in the greater scheme of things. We should be alert to the moment, flexible in our responses and willing to learn from our behavior. In short, we must be humble and practice humility in every situation and interpersonal encounter.

Dr. Gary Zukov writes <u>In the Seat of the Soul</u> (1999): "By striving for this reward and that reward, you ask the world to assess and acknowledge your value before you can value yourself. You place your sense of self-worth in the hands of others. You have no power even if you win every gold medal that the world can produce." He further writes that: "Humble spirits are free to love and to be who they are. They have no artificial standards to live up to. They are not drawn to symbols of external power. They do not compete for external power."

Dr. Wayne Dyer echoes this thought in <u>Wisdom of the Ages</u> (1998): ". . . the measure of greatness and happiness is the ability to subjugate the ego to the point of needing no credit for accomplishments, to be beyond needing gratitude or applause, to be independent of the good opinion of others, to just be doing what I do, because it is my purpose to do so." He goes on to say that once we stop needing the approval of others, a new kind of freedom is actualized. "Learn to live unseen and unknown, free of the need to be noticed."

In <u>Manifest Your Destiny</u> Dr. Dyer writes: "You are absolutely free when you are not consumed with your self importance. You are free when you no longer need to be stroked, coddled and approved of by everyone you meet. You are free when you are no longer offended by the actions of others (1999)."

Therefore, the key disposition to such a transformation is humility. Humility will allow us to begin perceiving our true nature, to look within and to rediscover ourselves. It will help us begin to find meaning and therefore freedom. Humility sustains as we strive to be more than we ever imagined.

C. <u>Humility and the issue control</u>

". . . you are wise and powerful, and no one else can help me,'
answered the Scarecrow.'" (<u>The Wizard of Oz</u>, 1900).

When you discover you have ultimate control over a few things and no control over many things you focus on that which you can change. You focus on the present, on the opportunity to express yourself and on taking responsibility for the consequences of your choices in the moment.

As we accept what we can't do, we contemplate what we can do. We marvel and trust in that which is the wonder of life, the Grand Plan. We embrace the awesome loving, yet frightening aspect of nature in general and our nature in particular. Becoming observers rather than managers is like going down your first roller coaster. It is extremely frightening yet when we get to the bottom we want to experience it again.

When we develop a humble perspective, we begin to realize and appreciate that in a unique way we are contributors and essential components of a benevolence that goes well beyond small, idiosyncratic wants and needs. We become empowered and free to love and cherish who we are without embellishment or deception. To be humble is to comprehend that the "I" (as ego and child self) is minimal and the "them" is nonexistent. To be humble and wise is to decide from a perspective of "we" and "us." It is to realize that you are one of the many who are one.

While we emerge from helplessness to empowerment, our focus changes from an external "blame" orientation to an internal, self-control orientation. With humility, we understand the changes we can make. We face vulnerability and build patience and trust in our source. From this perspective the illusory nature of the external's power is obvious therefore we search inward for solutions and truth. We come to embrace the authority of the self, the being who is generated internally and a reflection of our higher power. We renounce the dominance of the "child-self" which is based on external values and relies on the superficial for validation. This major shift of thought is necessary to achieve wellness and contentment.

D. <u>Humility enhances relationships</u>

"Humility, a sense of reverence before the sons of heaven . . ."
(Euripides, 485-406 BCE).

The traits herein are not mutually exclusive, rather they are mutually re-enforcing. Each characteristic merges and strengthens the others to create love, first for the "I" and then spreading to the "we," "us" and eventually decreasing the "them." After the progression from humility to gratitude, self-acceptance begins to dominate resulting in a well defined "I" who has the courage to encompass and embrace others without judgment or fear. Here we become free to be the "I" rather than to become the "I". We discover and embrace ourselves. This is how the practice of humility will reward and help establish relationships and love.

Your interactions with others are opportunities to show unconditional love and acceptance. For once, you can love with no hurt because there are no expectations of the other or yourself. You are free to be you. "They" are equally free. To compete is to strive for exclusion, to be "top dog" in others' eyes. To be humble, to love, to accept, is to embrace inclusion, to become the "we" and the "us." You are perfectly you and you are just where you should be in time and place. You are participating in and contributing to a wondrous, universal collaboration beyond your comprehension. Each day, each second, each encounter is an opportunity to learn and to contribute to the dance that is life. Relationships are the results of such dances.

E. **Summary**

Humility is the first step. From this spiritual quality springs all others. As we cultivate humility we develop a perspective which allows gratitude, trust, acceptance, wisdom, love and courage to blossom. Humility shines the light on our place in the Universe which in turn increases self-knowledge. As we learn about ourselves, we behave differently, prompting further learning. We begin to re-create, re-discover and re-assess initiating a freedom and contentment we've never known. We develop a new focus and thereby a greater efficiency in confronting change. Also we develop the courage to accept what we can't control. This acceptance and courage begins to reshape our relationships as the "we" and the "I" become equal.

IV. Impediments To Developing Humility

"We can't all be heroes because someone has
to sit on the curb and clap as they go by."
(Will Rogers, 1930).

A. Humility vs. consumerism

The attitudes of "me first," "I want," and "I deserve" significantly impair the ability to develop humility. In our culture, humility is frequently disparaged, often associated with low self-esteem, self-deprecation, as well as submissive, servile and sycophantic behavior. In short, to be humble is to be a loser.

Why is there such strong opposition to humility and respect when in other, more cooperative societies it is considered a virtue? The primary reason is that the culture of consumption is undermined when through humility we become empowered and free from external solutions. By renouncing the myth that we are deprived, deficient and/or defective, we corrode the very core of consumerism. If I am okay why do I need this product, utensil, and/or make over?

B. The myth of control

"'Why should I give you courage?' demanded Oz.
'Because of all Wizards you are the greatest, and alone
have power to grant my request,' answered the Lion.'"
(The Wizard of Oz, 1900).

Internally, the "child-self," which must always dominate in order to achieve satisfaction, will not go silently into the night. The notion that there is an external solution which is quick, easy and painless permeates the airwaves and drives the economy. If you are flawed, weak, or needy (and you are according to the mass media) there is a simple solution, which can be purchased in easy payments ("even if you have bad credit or no credit at all."). "Get what you deserve and make your life better," another broadcast bellows. This is an expression of arrogance and fear. Arrogance is the perspective that anything can be done if you only seek the external. Fear assumes that you can't tolerate the vulnerability that comes with patience, trusting your source and postponing gratification. The "child-self" craves immediate reward and will accept nothing else.

To counter this we must take a life changing step and practice humility. Being humble, we begin to tolerate unpleasant feelings of danger and uncertainty. We acknowledge and accept that a significant part of our lives (primarily the frivolous) is out of our control and that's okay. As we start to affirm this truth our life is transformed. Here is the essence of humility. As simple as this sounds it is not easy to attain. There are many commercial, economic, cultural and external impediments to such a perspective.

To resist the basic truth that we control little is to subject ourselves to a life of both personal and interpersonal strife. It is to pursue power where it cannot be achieved and to seek satisfaction where it cannot be attained. We are vulnerable to an existence of intrapersonal anarchy where addictions, compulsions, obsessions, harmful moods and/or impulsive behaviors reign. As we continue fruitless attempts at control, we create destructive relationships with friends, coworkers, family, lovers, authority figures, etc. To find peace we must surrender to and trust in a greater power.

C. <u>False pride</u>

"'Hush, my dear,' he said, 'don't speak so loud, or you will be overheard— and I should be ruined. I'm supposed to be a Great Wizard.'
'And aren't you?,' she asked.
'Not a bit of it, my dear; I'm just a common man.'"
<u>*(The Wizard of Oz,*</u> *1900).*

All of these reactions (anger, frustration, envy, fear etc.) are reflections of pride and hubris. According to many spiritual guides for more than 2,500 years, our true and only purpose in life is to grow in wisdom and love, while improving the lives of others. By practicing humility, we transform a small part of the universe into a place which reflects wisdom, love, and acceptance. Once we begin to trust and cultivate humility, we can embrace helplessness and assuage anxiety by knowing and acting on what can be controlled. We discover that we can master only the attitudes, feelings and actions in the moment. Although this is empowering, it is also an awesome responsibility and a daunting task.

As we begin our journey to growth, humility and trust, we'll become a more dominant player of life. Contentment and freedom will blossom and the child-self, with all its arrogance, narcissism and greed, will be replaced by a humble and loving person who will be at peace.

V. Summary

Humility is not easy to develop. As with all spiritual traits we must challenge early learning and the current cultural messages constantly impacting on our senses. When we increase awareness of our thinking and accept the internal as the center of control, we will more easily perfect all of the traits needed to grow in knowledge and spirit. While the external influence of culture impedes humility, we must also be aware of the child-self's internal tendency to be arrogant and presumptuous. Dominance by the child-self is simply another way of gaining a false sense of mastery and separating from our true nature. We create our prisons and humility is the key that will unlock our potential, releasing us to become who we are meant to be.

VI. For Further Consideration

1. Developing humility is the most important prelude to fostering the other spiritual traits (gratitude, patience/trust, acceptance) and achieving a life filled with growth and contentment.

2. To be humble is to be grounded, solid and reliable not passive, and humiliated.

3. To achieve humility is to understand and accept all that you can't control, thereby becoming empowered.

4. Humility generates the ability to be vulnerable and to trust, opening the way to mutually constructive interpersonal relationships.

5. Humility helps us focus and become aware of the role our higher power plays in life.

6. Humility helps us accept and embrace the perspective that life has a unique purpose and that we are an integral part of a plan far greater than ourselves.

7. An essential part of growth involves a basic perceptual shift from the child-self (ego) "I" "me" and "mine" to the more spiritual and ultimately more fulfilling "we," "us" and "ours."

8. The greatest act of humility is service to others.

9. Humility is the first step in our journey to

free ourselves from past myths and to recreate ourselves.

10. As we evolve and become exempt from the
"good opinion of others" we attain true
freedom and empowerment.

11. The culture of consumerism significantly
impedes awareness of the indispensable role
humility has in development.

12. In addition to social pressures hampering
humility, the child-self's natural pride,
arrogance and need for control hinders
spiritual progress.

Chapter 5

The Gift of Gratitude

"Gratitude is the fairest blossom which springs from the soul."

Henry Ward Beecher (1877).

I. Definitions

"If you will please take away the poll I shall be greatly obliged to you."

(*The Wizard of Oz*, 1900).

A. Current usage

The American Heritage Dictionary (4th edition) defines gratitude simply as "thankfulness" from the Latin word "gratus" meaning "pleasing." In turn "pleasing" is defined primarily as giving joy or satisfaction. Many current authors offer that "gratitude" is associated with feelings of completeness, fulfillment and adequacy. Others view "gratitude" as the response when one receives a gift. They all agree that gratitude requires an awareness or acknowledgement of one party about the beneficial action of another. As Dr. Ladner (2004) writes: "Etymologically, the word 'grateful' implies a feeling of fullness and thankfulness for all that is great in others and in ourselves."

B. Gratitude and the four pillars of contentment

"Gratitude is not only the greatest of virtues but the parent of all others." (Cicero, 21 BCE). Gratitude stems from humility and adds to the development of the other two spiritual and mental traits necessary for growth and contentment viz. patience/trust and acceptance. If we take nothing for granted and truly understand our role in the universe we will develop humility. From this perspective we are appreciative and more aware of the bounty that infuses our lives. This is a working definition of gratitude.

From the awareness of such gifts, and that they arise less from our own action than the good will of others and the beneficence of the universe comes the conclusion that we can trust in the future and that we are part of a loving design. Therefore when events are contrary to expectation and may cause distress and inconvenience, it is logical to trust that such events happen for a reason and that ultimately all will be well. We need not act. We need only to be patient and allow events to unfold. As such, the third pillar of contentment, acceptance, becomes the appropriate perspective for all circumstances which we encounter in our daily lives.

C. Gratitude and acceptance

Gratitude and acceptance are reciprocal qualities. If we accept life on life's terms as well as our ability to cope with events, our self-esteem will grow. As it grows, it propagates even greater acceptance of ourselves and others which then increases our gratitude. Each of the four pillars (humility, gratitude, acceptance, patience) reinforces and invigorates the others resulting in a mutually beneficial cycle of growth, the ultimate result being a life of contentment and satisfaction.

Gratitude and acceptance guide us to enjoying what is, rather than what should be. They promote contentment and decrease the urge to seek an external cure when we experience unpleasant feelings. We become grateful for the moment because we accept life as it is.

D. <u>Gratitude and courage</u>

We can only be as grateful as we are courageous. It takes courage to open ourselves to new experiences and to find a purpose in that which challenges us. It takes courage to be vulnerable and to realize that we are dependent on others to complete ourselves. It also takes courage to face society without excuses, regrets or criticisms. Courage allows us to face the world with behaviors that reflect our belief system. It is courage that puts our ideas to the test and helps us confront life and achieve our dreams. Be grateful for courage and be sufficiently courageous to be grateful.

E. <u>Summary</u>

"If you see no reason for giving thanks, the fault lies in yourself."
(American Indian Proverb).

To summarize, the gratitude expressed here is born of humility and love. It embraces the realization that we are special and that we have an incomparable gift to offer everyone we meet. All that we have and all that we do is for the purpose of sharing this gift and fulfilling our destiny.

Gratitude helps us understand that success is helping others achieve. Real satisfaction resides in giving and not in acquiring external goods or power. To be grateful is to begin to crack the shell of the egg that is "I" and to allow someone to enter and share our individuality. It is to open ourselves to others in order to become an "us" and to rejoice in all that ensues. To be grateful is to be self-less while maintaining a firm understanding and cherishing of the self.

Gratitude is a gift from God to help us celebrate life. It transforms life into a work of art which we create through love. It destroys depression because it frees us from our self-pity and self-involvement as we become thankful for all that is and all that we are. We then understand that despite our faults and blemishes we are perfectly us.

Humility is the catalyst for gratitude as gratitude catalyzes patience, acceptance and love. To be grateful is to be patient, to trust that our destiny is unfolding and to accept the unexpected while embracing the journey that is life.

To adhere to these principles is to create a perspective in which every day is challenging, fun, fulfilling and enlightening. We are grateful in knowing that God makes no mistakes. Be in the moment, be aware and witness every miracle around you. Give what you can and receive with love and humility. "Be silent of the services you have rendered, but speak of the favors you have received." (Seneca, 47 CE).

II. The Role of Gratitude In Everyday Life

"If the only prayer you ever said in your life was 'thank you', that would suffice."

(Meister Eckhart, 1297).

A. Gratitude as a daily gift

". . . and behold! Here was the Scarecrow, as good as ever, thanking them over and over for saving him." (The Wizard of Oz, 1900).

How can developing gratitude in our daily routines lead to total fulfillment? To appreciate what we have, to savor each moment, to wonder and experience all of life's gifts is to realize we are part of a larger plan. According to Marianne Willamson (2002), "Gratitude is essential to happiness. Developing a grateful attitude knowing that every time we arrive somewhere safely, we have something to be happy about; every time our children rush up to us and smile, we have something to be happy about…that is the essence of a happy existence. Happiness is a muscle we must use, or it will wither away." Gratitude is the exercise we need to energize that muscle. Life is a force which we can resist or embrace. This is our choice. If we are to achieve our absolute potential, we must be willing to witness, submit to and respect all that we can't control. To be grateful is to be part of this process because it amplifies our awareness of all possibilities and cushions disappointments.

Respecting ourselves sufficiently that we have the strength to embrace another is a goal which has to be pursued. To see in each instance a personal message of love and acceptance as well as a call to develop is the blessing of the universe on the individual. To be most effective, gratitude like the other three pillars, requires courage. Courage opens our eyes. It allows us to acknowledge (but not necessarily accept) our faults and to make them strengths. Courage is saying "I love you" to ourselves, to others and to life. Courage is assessing our vulnerabilities and understanding that this act, in itself, makes us stronger. It takes courage to be grateful because to be grateful we need humility.

B. <u>Gratitude and self-esteem</u>

"'Thank you very much', said the Scarecrow, when he had been set down on the ground. 'I feel like a new man.'"
(<u>The Wizard of Oz</u>, 1900).

Gratitude is a gift to the self. Of the four pillars generating and supporting love, wisdom and courage it is the one which fills us with a sense of appreciation and affinity for life and all it has to offer. We feel and believe that we are just where we should be, that our trials and challenges are unique opportunities to learn and grow. We feel and believe that we are perfect, but with faults which help us and the community learn and grow in love. We know that strengths are spawned by these faults. We are special with particular talents which we offer to humanity. This perspective enhances self-esteem. The gift of gratitude embodies appreciating and cherishing all life forms in addition to the exquisite components of daily living. It is the best antidote to depression and low self-esteem. Cultivating gratitude makes each day exceptional and joyful.

The theory of cognitive dissonance states that you cannot hold two contrary ideas or feelings in your consciousness simultaneously. Therefore, it is impossible to believe and experience that you are deprived, deficient and defective while also feeling grateful for who you are, for what you have, and for your ability to uniquely contribute to the world around you.

C. Gratitude as a gift from God

Gratitude is truly a gift from God. It frequently arises in our awareness without any intent or effort on our part. It is something we must be open to in order to receive. It allows us to treasure each moment and each experience. A sunset, a smiling face, a familiar song, the touch of velvet on your skin, are all noticed, enhanced and enjoyed due to gratitude.

Gratitude is to life and our growth what rain is to flowers, and what flowers are to spring. We cannot reach the goal of contentment without the spiritual quality of gratitude. Yet our will alone will never help us capture this feeling. Rather it is the result of humility, trust and acceptance that allows both the awareness and the fullness of this sensation.

Gratitude is a product of surrender to a greater plan. This requires a trust and a belief that the universe is beneficent, bestowing on us exactly what we need when we need it. Similar to each of the four pillars of contentment, it reinforces the others in a reciprocal dance of understanding and unity. To be gratified is to be indulged, to be pleased and to be satisfied. When we are grateful we both give and receive pleasure.

Ultimately, gratitude is granted by a higher power to enhance the qualities (love, acceptance, humility, patience, courage and wisdom) necessary to achieve fulfillment. It is a gift to be cherished, nurtured, accepted and acknowledged. It can be felt and brought to awareness in each moment. Each interaction, incitement and accomplishment is an occasion to feel and profess gratitude. Gratitude is an opportunity to savor the instant and simultaneously to realize with humility that this time would not have occurred without a confluence of the self and a higher power.

We cannot be grateful without acknowledging the contributions of others. Althea Gibson remarked that her every achievement was inspired, effected or spawned by another. Sir Isaac Newton wrote: "We stand on the shoulders of giants." Gratitude unites and reminds us that we are all precious and contributors to the growth of others. We can learn from anyone and we can be examples to all.

D. Gratitude and relationships

"Gratitude is the antidote to bitterness and resentment."
(M.J. Ryan, 1999)

"If it wasn't for Dorothy I should never had brains. She lifted me from the pole in the cornfield and brought me to the Emerald City. So my good luck is all due to her, and I shall never leave her until she starts back to Kansas for good and all."
(Scarecrow, The Wizard of Oz, 1900).

Gratitude is at the core of good relationships whether close (emotionally or geographically) or distant. When we are grateful for those who play a role in our lives, we rise above petty judgments and fill both our hearts and theirs with love.

Buddhism strongly emphasizes that we exist interdependently.

Dr. Lorne Ladner (2004) writes : "We, all, are inextricably connected by complex relations of casualty. Denying interdependence means that we deny who we are and how we actually exist. Healthy individuation allows for a compassionate, mature sense of ethics, taking responsibility for how our actions affect others." (p. 170). "Injustice anywhere is a threat to justice everywhere. We are caught in an inescapable network of mutuality, tied in a single garment of destiny. Whatever affects one directly, affects all indirectly," wrote Martin Luther King Jr.

Gratitude allows us to appreciate who we are, where we come from and who helped us get here. If we are content now with our current circumstances, we must be grateful for those who helped us through our trials and tribulations as well as those who helped us focus and persevere in order to get to this place. Humility allows us to accept this and gratitude is humility's expression. It manifests thanks and appreciation. To develop relationships and contentment, it is essential that we reflect on and acknowledge the kindness and good deeds we have received in the past. Feeling and expressing gratitude adds spirit to our life as well as the lives of those who have helped us.

Ladner (2004) continues this thought by reminding us that "object relations analysts also note that thinking of others with gratitude allows us to identify with them and to internalize the love and kindness they've shown us, enhancing our ability to feel good about ourselves and to feel love for others" (p. 167). It helps open our hearts by reducing fear and increasing trust, patience and acceptance.

M. J. Ryan (1999) points out that when it comes to the behavior of others, there's little we can predict or control because there are too many variables. Therefore, we can't take for granted anything someone does for us. Realizing this increases gratitude and we begin to treasure all the shared moments. One of gratitude's most important gifts is fostering this sense of connection.

E. Gratitude and giving

"So they oiled his legs until he could move then freely; and he thanked them again and again for his release, for he seemed a very polite creature, and very grateful." (The Wizard of Oz, 1900).

Gratitude allows us to give and receive without shame or false pride. Whether materially, emotionally or behaviorally we can share and rejoice in our connection with others. We shed the veneer of rugged individuality and revel in mutuality and trust. We celebrate our commonalities and reject our differences. Each day, each action becomes a gift which we both give and receive. With gratitude, love is allowed to flow freely between and among all who participate.

The art of giving and receiving is an essential aspect of all relationships, namely, how much of "me" do I give to create and enhance the "us". It's important to remember that just as much love is expressed in receiving as in giving. Both parties share in this joyous and selfless dynamic and both are rewarded. Any type of gift will do: an object, a favor, a compliment, a kind thought. Forgiveness and acceptance may be the greatest of gifts with the greatest mutual rewards. Love requires such active and passive behaviors and therein lies its reciprocity.

In each moment there is an opportunity to both give and receive. It is an opportunity to mature and to better understand and accept ourselves and our world. Everyday we can offer those we meet the unique gift of ourselves and we can receive, in turn, their singularity and good will. With this perspective we are able to see each interaction as a chance for development, acceptance and a mutual celebration of life.

F. Summary

Gratitude is necessary for happiness, improvement and satisfaction. Each day, the opportunity to be grateful presents itself and we must open our hearts to this awareness. It increases self-esteem because we see the good in ourselves and our actions.

We begin to feel and believe that we are perfectly us with flaws that enhance our individuality. These flaws can be used for enrichment and as an incentive to direct our lives on a path of compassion and contentment.

The nectar of humility is gratitude. As we cultivate the first, the latter is intensified and infuses itself in all areas. Gratitude can be felt and brought into awareness, every moment of our lives. It strengthens relationships because it exhorts us to prize and cherish those who chose to share our lives. It allows us to give and receive in an acknowledgement of mutuality and respect.

III. Gratitude As a Positive Life Force

A. Developing gratitude adds joy to our daily life

"Life will bring you pain all by itself. Your responsibility is to create joy."

(Milton Erickson, M.D.).

Gratitude allows us to enjoy every minute of life, every interaction and experience if we only open our hearts. As we develop this gift, we will come to understand that there is no limit to the abundance which surrounds us.

Each day it is important to expand our awareness of the blessings we have as well as the burdens that we don't. As a form of prayer, during different parts of the day, we should pause to think of our good fortune and enjoy the feeling of well being which this thought engenders. Such an act will connect us to the divine and amplify feelings of contentment. Remember that not only do roses have thorns but thorns have roses.

As you become grateful for the gifts in the present you find that resenting past events makes no sense because it was precisely those situations and individuals which led you to the place you are now and now is the best it can be. Thusly, our perspective changes from the narrow view of want, need and resentment to the more encompassing view of satisfaction, fulfillment and forgiveness.

According to Dr. Wayne Dyer in, There's a Spiritual Solution to Every Problem, (2001): "Finding joy means consciously deciding to process your life in ways that focus on gratefulness for what you have. You can cultivate this attitude by refusing to allow yourself to think in terms of scarcity. Being joyful means thinking joyful thoughts, even when you are tempted otherwise." He goes on to write: "The habit of thinking in sorrowful ways is a result of your training. You learned (emphasis by this author) that joy was possible only when life was going the way you thought it should. Consequently, you developed a habit of abandoning a joyful, appreciative thought in favor of sadness when life wasn't as you thought it should be. . ."

Again the issue is one of control. As Dr. Dyer implies when our plans are thwarted we are taught that this is bad rather than an opportunity to learn and progress. As we develop the other pillars of contentment namely humility, patience/trust and acceptance we will understand that a divine plan supersedes any plan that we may have and that when our aims are hindered it is an opportunity to re-think and re-group.

IV. Impediments to Gratitude

*"Be content with what you have; rejoice in the way things are.
When you realize there is nothing lacking, the whole world
belongs to you." (Lao Tzu, 6th century BC).*

A. Gratitude and responsibility

One of the most significant impediments to gratitude is a clinging, love affair with our past which keeps us wed to the status quo and enslaved by a negative self-image. This prevents us from re-creating ourselves and moving forward. Despite feelings and instincts that tell us to change and move on, we justify our gridlock by recalling myths from the past and continue our self-destructive pattern of doing the same thing but expecting different results.

By reducing regret and resentment in the present, gratitude helps us appreciate the past despite its sordid and destructive aspects. At the very least, we survived and learned new skills in order to move on. By acquiring gratitude, we cherish who we are now and cannot, according to the theory of cognitive dissonance, simultaneously denigrate our past. If we are chained to the past, know that we, and we alone, have the keys to free ourselves.

The events and the individuals who are part of our history are the primary powers which defined who we are and where we are in the quest to fulfill our destiny. As we cultivate gratitude and appreciation for today, we inevitably become grateful for yesterday and thereby release ourselves from regret, resentment and reproach. We move on with our lives liberated from the obligation of pleasing others.

B. Self-pity

Another significant obstacle to fostering gratitude is the tendency to wallow in self-pity. This can be quite tempting because we easily adopt a shield of helplessness to avoid a sword of responsibility. "I can't," "I would but . . . ," "if only . . . ," etc., will keep us stagnated and content with mediocrity and debilitation. But how can you be grateful today if you are hungry, alone, broke and tired? The truth is that we constrain ourselves by choosing an area of fixation. Therefore, we can be emancipated from toxic thoughts and feelings by having the courage to confront them and change. Through a lens of gratitude, we can then envision our role in promoting compassion and service rather than indulging in a narrow focus of impotence and incompetence, desire and deficiency.

There will always be a time in our life when we encounter a mental wall that is both too imposing to surmount and too expansive to circumvent. During these moments if we focus on abundance and gratitude, we will create the courage to change our perspective to one of competence and fulfillment. What we have in any point of time is what we need to achieve and if we avoid the pitfalls of self-pity we will create a solution to every problem. By staying focused, separating from the past and our preconceived notions of failure, we can be filled with joy and generate an awareness of the bounty that surrounds us. When all else fails, serve others and your spirit will soar.

C. Our culture of deficiency and want

"Oz, left to himself, smiled to think of his success in giving the Scarecrow, the Tin Woodman, and the Lion exactly what they thought they wanted. 'How can I help being a humbug?' he said, 'when all these people make me do things that everybody knows can't be done?'" (The Wizard of Oz, 1900).

Once again our culture of narcissism and obsessive consumption prevents us from attaining our goal of contentment and self-awareness. As Mitch Albom writes: "'We've got a form of brainwashing going on in our country,' Morrie sighed. 'Do you know how they brainwash people? They repeat something over and over. And that's what we do in this country. Owning things is good. More money is good. More property is good. More commercialism is good. *More is good. More is good.* We repeat it and have it repeated to us – over and over until nobody bothers to think otherwise.'" (Mitch Albom, Tuesdays with Morrie, 1997).

Dr. Lorne Ladner (2004) concurs: "The advertising we're exposed to daily, also tends to lead us away from feelings of gratitude...", they are designed to make us feel impaired, inadequate and/or incomplete. The purpose of advertising is to propagate "wants" not needs. Thus begins a cycle of useless consumption leading to constant disappointment, frustration, resentment and fear. We are robbed of the gift of gratitude, of savoring what we have. Instead, we focus on what we don't have. The only way for consumerism to thrive is to obliterate the potential for gratitude. Once we appreciate what we have and understand that we have all we need, we stop spending, stop feeling deficient and stop looking outside to fix that which is not broken.

D. The culture of false independence

Gratitude is also thwarted by the cultural ideal of independence, the self-made person. It states that what we have, we earned through our own efforts, with no ones' help. This is well illustrated by the myth of the "Marlboro Man" riding alone in the west, rugged and self-sufficient, independent (except for his need to smoke) and self-assured. This is the ideal. If we have a certain car, wristwatch, running shoe etc. we are complete, we need no one and we are the envy of all. Objects destroy unity and intimacy offering a fraudulent sense of power and control. There is no place for gratitude or humility. No place for the truth that what we have and who we are is based on a long line of others whose good will and blessings have helped us thrive. When we consider the idea that many people have participated in and contributed to our life, we experience the joy of connectedness, trust and humility. We no longer have to look elsewhere. Feelings of isolation and vulnerability disappear, replaced by gratitude, approval, and association.

But in order to realize this we must embrace change. This is a daunting task in which we must attempt to neutralize formidable forces. We have to develop a new attitude and a new perspective. It requires time and patience. Our goal and our intent is to focus on affirmation rather than exclusion, potential rather than helplessness. Such thinking is anathema to our culture and economy. To achieve contentment we must change. We should seek inclusion, acceptance, humility, and love in our religion, our family and in all the power that is greater than we. Without others we cannot survive.

E. <u>Our reflexive rejection of gratitude</u>

Dr. Robert Karen in <u>The Forgiving Self</u> (2001) writes that the "…stubborn, unconscious unwillingness to feel gratitude falls into the class of terrible things we do to ourselves. In rejecting it, we deny ourselves one of the fundamental pleasures of love." He continues with the basic premise that there are multiple reasons not to feel gratitude rooted in our environment as well as in ourselves. He cites one example where to feel gratitude would mean to give up the power of feeling resentment. Hence, gratitude implies a surrender and a vulnerability. Most of us are more comfortable surrounded by barriers or walls, which isolate us while offering a manufactured sense of power, control and dominance.

When we feel gratitude we credit the "other" with giving us what we lack. Without trust in our capabilities, such a situation forces us back to dependency and weakness. According to Karen (2001), if I am small and weak, as acknowledged by gratitude, you are large and powerful and I am at your mercy. Therefore to experience gratitude we must expose ourselves to vulnerability and strip ourselves of the illusion of self-sufficiency. We must realize that we are, in fact, helpless without others. As M.J. Ryan writes in, <u>Attitudes of Gratitude (1999)</u>: "Openheartedness takes courage. It requires enough trust in the goodness of other people and the universe to put aside our self-protectiveness."

We must strive to remember the daily kindnesses and respect that are part of our lives. As we harvest gratitude, feelings of happiness, connectedness, fullness and serenity will become palpable. Dr. Ladner (2004) observes that when we cultivate a temperament of gratitude we will realize that we are "the recipient and receptacle of limitless love and kindness." By nurturing a sincere and powerful sense of gratitude we move beyond self-defeating tendencies.

V. Summary

"I have been very kindly treated in your lovely City, and everyone has been good to me. I cannot tell you how grateful I am."
(Dorothy to the Guardian, The Wizard of Oz, 1900).

Gratitude, similar to the other pillars of contentment must be practiced daily to be properly and fully enriched. Make an effort to increase your awareness of the abundance of love and good will that encompasses you. Each night remind yourself of the blessings you have been given. Don't ignore what is, for what could or should be. Don't allow shortcomings to squash skills. Stay in the moment and focus on the now as you feel gratitude grow.

Gratitude is the logical extension of humility and the prelude to patience, trust, acceptance and forgiveness, as we realize that what we have is good and that the universe is both bountiful and beneficent. Such a compassionate cosmos must be trusted to shelter and support us.

Gratitude is a gift that gives us joy and optimism. It promotes progress during difficult times because we recognize that events could be worse and that we have been given many blessings. Gratitude allows us to treasure life and conquer fear. It is to feel our higher power embracing us as we join humanity in pursuing our destiny and materializing our goal of expanding love.

VI. For Further Consideration

1. Gratitude is the second pillar of development which serves as a precondition for contentment and a precursor to acceptance and patience.

2. Gratitude is the logical extension of humility, the first pillar of contentment.

3. Gratitude embraces the realization that we are special and that we have a unique gift to offer others.

4. Gratitude is a gift from God to celebrate our lives. It serves to nurture and catalyze the other spiritual attitudes that comprise contentment.

5. Gratitude mitigates depression because it frees us from self-pity and self-involvement.

6. Gratitude resides in the present while regret resides in the past.

7. Gratitude is an essential quality for happiness and successful relationships.

8. The gift of gratitude embodies appreciating and cherishing others in addition to the smallest details of our daily lives.

9. Gratitude and courage help us acknowledge and revere our interdependence.

10. Gratitude allows us to give and receive without false pride and shame.

11. Gratitude helps us relinquish resentments and re-write the past in a more positive, self-enhancing way.

12. Gratitude promotes acceptance of what is while minimizing the "shoulds", "woulds" and "coulds."

13. Gratitude is impeded by fear and arrogance as well as our innate desire to maintain the status quo.

14. Gratitude is thwarted by self pity and the cultural demands for consumption.

15. Gratitude is antithetical to feelings of deprivation, deficiency and depression.

16. Gratitude eschews isolation and embraces inclusion and interdependence.

17. To receive the gift of gratitude we must be open to transformation and fearless of change.

18. To deny ourselves the gift of gratitude is to deny ourselves one of the fundamental pleasures of life.

Chapter 6

Acceptance
The Art of Surrender

"All pain comes from a futile search for what you want, insisting that it must be."

(A Course in Miracles, 1976).

". . . and I am thankful I am made of straw and cannot be easily damaged. There are worse things in the world than being a Scarecrow." (The Wizard of Oz, 1900).

I. Definitions

To "accept" has a variety of nuanced uses but the most relevant would be:

> A. to "believe in the goodness of something"
> (i.e. to acknowledge, affirm, approve).

B. to "put up with," "to go along with" (i.e. to capitulate, defer to, endure, submit suffer, tolerate, yield to).

C. "to agree or consent to" (i.e. to admit, adopt, undertake).

The word "accept" itself comes for the Latin "acceptare" or "accipere" which translated means "to take something to oneself."

From this we can derive both an active and passive use:

1. active (viz. "to believe in," " to agree/consent to")

2. passive (viz. "to put up with," "to defer," " to go along with")

Both uses are relevant in our pursuit of growth and contentment. The Serenity Prayer speaks of "accepting" that which we can't change. Here we "defer, "go along with" or "defer to" but we don't manage or direct. We step back and let our higher power do the work. We suspend control and attempts to manage the status quo. Instead of administrating, we "put up with" that which is external and beyond our control.

In its active form "acceptance" also guides us in the direction of growth and contentment. In this form we make an active decision in the here and now to "believe in" or "consent to" the plan of our higher power. We make a commitment to the concept that if we surrender and trust in the goodness of the universe we will achieve all that we were meant to achieve. Hence, both the active and the passive forms of acceptance are critical components for our journey to self-fulfillment.

Dr. Wayne Dyer (1998) writes: "Once when I was asked to define 'enlightenment' the best I could come up with was "the quiet acceptance of 'what is.'" Truly enlightened beings are those who refuse to allow themselves to be distressed over things that simply are the way they are. "If we are to achieve our goals of contentment and growth we must conquer our mental tendency to relate all present situations and events either to the past or the future. Contentment and growth are found in the moment." (Dyer, 1999).

A. Acceptance and the Serenity Prayer

"O God, give us serenity to accept what cannot be changed . . ."
(Reinhold Niebuhr, 1934).

Such "acceptance" is combined with the qualities of "courage" and "wisdom" found in the Serenity Prayer. Here we ask for the ability to "accept" what we can't change. The difficulty is that the "child-self" or ego fears the vulnerability which arises when we acknowledge our lack of omnipotence. The truth is that we consciously control very little of our internal thoughts, feelings and actions and almost nothing that occurs outside of us. However, with awareness and intent we can begin to master the former and with patience, trust and humility we can begin to tolerate, and accept the latter and its attendant emotional distress.

Ultimately, as we progress we will acquire the ability to think, feel and act differently. Transforming our perspective will alter our reactions to events which in turn will modify external reactions to us. Acceptance is not passivity. Instead it is an active and purposeful decision to surrender. As Dr. Dyer (1995) writes: "acceptance is not endorsement but rather it relieves us of the internal stress of trying to control something that is beyond our powers and abilities. It allows us to peacefully observe such events as they unfold." Under these circumstances acceptance generates reflection and contributes to empowerment. We can now focus on our internal state in addition to the current thoughts and feelings we can control.

B. Acceptance and empowerment

"In the adaptability and ease with which we experience change lie our happiness and freedom." (Buddha, c. 510 BC).

We recreate and rebuild our character by living in the moment, being aware in that moment and making choices about that which we control. We create who we are and what our future will be, one moment and one decision at a time.

Acceptance generates such creativity and empowerment because we allow ourselves to be whoever we are, absent of judgments and preconceptions. We are perfectly us with all our shortcomings. Yet we always strive with love and compassion to be better because that is our objective as well as our reward.

C. Self-acceptance as a developmental process

"We cannot change anything until we accept it."
(Carl Gustav Jung, 1910).

Similar to all the qualities noted here, self-acceptance is a progression. It involves maturation, learning, trial, and error. As always, we need awareness of this process and intent to examine new situations and the role we play in these situations. From this we assess our strengths and weaknesses and we are then prepared to alter perspectives and approaches for the next challenge.

It is unlikely that we will achieve total self-acceptance as we strive for improvement. This can be both frustrating and debilitating. However, it is possible to avoid self-condemnation. Instead of negative self-talk, we should begin to relish our individuality and continuing development as we evaluate each new interaction and obstacle. Fear, judgment, false pride and self-destructive thoughts are proclivities which impede improvement towards self-acceptance. We must "let go" of these and begin to attain love, courage, trust and humility which will make achieving self-acceptance much easier. Such characteristics will also lead to compassion. Compassion is feeling and acknowledging that we are united with all humankind in both talents and faults.

D. Self-acceptance and learning

"The best thing to do when it's raining is to let it rain."
(Henry Wadsworth Longfellow, 1862).

In order to grow, we must learn from mistakes. This is the path to knowledge and wisdom. We best learn from our mistakes by accepting our strengths and vulnerabilities. Each event which enters awareness is meaningful because it is an opportunity to learn. There are no random events, each and every event has a meaning which only we can decipher and understand. However, we have to develop the perspective that to discover our path we stay in the moment and allow our higher power to guide us.

E. Summary

"Everyone seemed happy and contented and prosperous." (Dorothy's observation about the residents of the Emerald City,
The Wizard of Oz, 1900).

Acceptance is one of four essential spiritual qualities that must be developed and used in our daily lives if we are to achieve the goals of growth and contentment. The other three are humility, gratitude and patience/trust. Taken together these four provide the foundation for love, courage, and wisdom, the primary spiritual qualities necessary for a life of contentment. Dr. Wayne Dyer (1998) considers this "enlightenment" and The Serenity Prayer invokes acceptance as the first spiritual quality necessary to achieve serenity.

The central challenge is to transform our thinking in order to distinguish what we can and can't control in our lives. Unfortunately, we carry with us the delusion that we manage many things and regulate numerous outside occurrences. A significant source of emotional distress and adversarial social interaction originates with this delusion. In truth, we must uncover and ascertain what we do and do not control. Acquiring acceptance and humility is crucial to future development and social maturation.

II. Other Manifestations of Acceptance

"Every person, no matter who, can be the teacher we need, if instead of judging, we listen, accept, and love."
(Buddha, c. 540 BC).

A. Unconditional love

As Marianne Williamson writes in A Return to Love (1992): "Any situation that pushes our buttons is a situation where we don't yet have the capacity to love unconditionally." For Carl Rogers (1961) unconditional love or unconditional positive regard was the cornerstone of his approach to psychotherapy. If the client believed and felt that the therapist heard the client's concerns and accepted him/her without qualifications or reservations, treatment would be successful. For Rogers the key to success was that the self-loathing patient finally encountered someone who respected, embraced and affirmed them even with their darkest secrets.

Unconditional love and unconditional positive regard are synonymous with acceptance. As it applies to our daily lives, unconditional love is about adopting the notion that we are one of God's creatures and part of the human race, destined to participate in a plan greater than ourselves. We are all on a journey and we are all reflections of God's love. If obstacles are met with patience, trust and courage they will be overcome for the benefit of all.

If we believe the premise that God created us and that we

are as we should be despite faults and deficits, self-acceptance follows. We start to see that we are loveable and we begin to appreciate all that we are as we diminish thoughts of what we are not. Once we achieve this, approbation of others and the world in general will follow. We will embrace the idea that we are one with all and that we have everything we need to achieve satisfaction and respect.

B. Acceptance and love

"Love is not love which alters when it alteration finds."
(Shakespeare, 1609).

Humility, acceptance, forgiveness, gratitude, trust and patience are primary components of love. If we are to achieve destiny's goal of expanding love and joy we must try to honor and empathize with others. Acceptance is an essential component of The Serenity Prayer because in order to achieve the contentment and serenity life has to offer we must value and acknowledge ourselves and our circumstances. We must define what we can't do and assume the obligation to change the things we can. In this prayer we also request the courage and wisdom which is necessary to accomplish this. In his prayer, Reinhold Niebuhr (1892 – 1971) offers the most succinct and profound advice to living a spiritually and emotionally fulfilling life. It is one of the best guides to psychological health and should be recited throughout the day as we encounter new situations and life's travails.

If you want to be accepted and loved you must accept and love. To achieve this we need to practice forgiveness. "Forgive us our trespasses as we forgive those who trespass against us." (The Lord's Prayer). "It is in forgiving that we are forgiven, for it is in giving that we receive." (St. Francis of Assisi 1181-1226).

C. Acceptance and humility

"What is done for you—allow it to be done."
(Ibrahim Ibn Al-Khawwas, 9th century C.E.).

By achieving and developing this temperament of tolerance, we start to see every event and every encounter as the road to a new, more rewarding life. It is an opportunity to learn and grow. We gradually depersonalize life experiences and realize that we are only the witness to the event and not the event itself. We distance ourselves and undertake the perspective of the scientist (participant/observer). In this manner, impulsivity is reduced significantly while personal control is expanded and reinforced. We now have the capacity to hesitate before acting. In effect, we stop the flow of time, pause and assess prior to choosing reactions and emotions. Hence, our perspective is modified and we thereby recreate ourselves.

Humility teaches us that we can learn from anyone during any encounter. When you have an open, accepting perspective a mentor will appear. The universe and everything therein becomes a tutor for all of life's wonders. We begin to understand our place in the grand plan and our responsibility in creating a new order.

D. Acceptance and strength

"Acceptance of what has happened is the first step to overcoming the consequences of any misfortune." (William James, 1879).

Similar to humility, acceptance does not mean that we are passive or disempowered. In fact, the opposite is true. Acceptance is a sign of strength. It is the ability to look at the current situation and to move forward without judgment, self-pity, blame or fear. Acceptance acknowledges what we can and can't master. It strengthens us because we become focused on those areas which we can realistically alter. It takes strength to give up the delusion of mastery and to put our fate in the hands of an unknown power. It takes strength to trust. However, once we understand the limits of our domination and influence, we begin to move forward with confidence. We are responsible for our actions and reactions but we cannot always be in control of the results or the events which precipitated our behavior. We cannot regulate what happens only how we respond behaviorally and emotionally. Therefore, it is essential that when we act we intend only love and compassion.

E. Summary

There are many ways to manifest and advance acceptance as we face the daily challenges of life. One way is to show compassion for others by listening and loving them without judgment. To cease blaming and to attempt serving is a blessed action that benefits both ourselves and another.

If we have true humility, we realize that we are cherished by our higher power despite our lack of perfection. We now must understand that others are in the same position and that we have no right to judge or blame. As we accept ourselves, we are able to make an active decision to accept others as they are. When we achieve this we will feel gratification with an intensity as never before.

III. How We Resist Acceptance

A. Projection and fear hampering acceptance

"The secret of health for both mind and body is not to mourn for the past, worry about the future, or anticipate troubles, but to live in the present moment wisely and earnestly."
(The Buddha, c. 563- 483 BC).

Both projection and fear will hamper any attempt at change or growth and therefore will prevent contentment. Fear of the unknown, (especially of change), lack of trust and lack of self-control, all contribute to immobility. We tend to justify maintaining the status quo yet it is what prevents moving forward. When faced with this we minimize the distress and dysfunction of the present and we continue to suffer. "If it ain't broke don't fix it" becomes our motto but in our heart we know that it is badly broken.

Projection is used as a justification for fear. With projection we don't have to acknowledge our fear rather we hide behind it using the word "caution." Projection is the great "what if." Before we begin any new action, fear intrudes and stops us by asking a variety of "what if" questions, the answer to which portend doom and failure. There are times when such caution is appropriate and we must carefully evaluate our thinking under these circumstances. But frequently caution is an excuse for inaction and a significant impediment to growth.

So don't project. Evaluate the challenge with each new step or fact as you move forward. "Before freaking out, wait to the end of the story." M.J. Ryan (2004) advises. Don't assume or presume, rather begin action slowly and invoke The Serenity Prayer.

Having the patience and trust to allow the process to evolve:

1. Eliminates projection and catastrophizing ("what if" exaggerated to the extreme degree). You stop worrying about all that could go wrong.

2. Lets you step back, pause and evaluate how your efforts are unfolding and how the results fit into your overall goal. This will give you a fresh and optimistic perspective which in turn will make you more relaxed and confident as you proceed.

B. <u>Consumerism versus acceptance</u>

"The Lion would have preferred a bed of dried leaves in the forest, and did not like being shut up in a room; but he had too much sense to let this worry him . . ." (The Wizard of Oz, 1900).

As with many traits we need in order to achieve growth and contentment, acceptance is hampered and vilified by the consumer culture. The credo of consumerism is that you are defective, deficient or deprived and something can fix you. This hampers growth in all areas because acquisitions become solutions and you become addicted to the external for the "fix." The "fix" is an anesthetic which clouds your view of reality while soothing the pain that the child-self feels for being deprived and ignored. Instead of discovering the real you which is the true source of power, you become that which you own. When you feel empty you yearn for more "stuff" not realizing that you can never get enough of what you don't need. As you acquire more and more, the emptiness remains but instead of causing you to stop, you continue to consume in the hope that one day, one thing, will make you content.

The fact is you are just as you should be and no number of external objects is going to change that. Yes you have flaws but they are a part of your God given character. The mission to improve these blemishes is an ingredient of the "Grand Plan" through which you are recreated and rejuvenated.

Consumerism wants you to be an addict of consumption. Addiction is craving something you don't need. The consumer culture tells us what we require and masks the distinction between desires and needs. It indoctrinates the perfect you to become dependent and damaged. In reality, consumerism creates, amplifies and disguises wants as needs. Similar to the difference between lust and love we blindly move forward with a fixation to amass more and as a result we mortgage our true nature in order to have the most recent gadget or immediate satisfaction.

Acceptance changes this self-destructive dance. It puts a barrier between the cultural exultations and messages that we are deficient and the truth that we are as God made us and we have all that is necessary for fulfillment. Acceptance fights the false belief that if we can only acquire some thing we will become content, satisfied and respected. To fight these destructive and disempowering messages takes courage and trust. Our initial response to such a challenge is stress, fear, and uncertainty. Acceptance of the challenge, trust in the outcome and faith in the future will help us achieve contentment. Accept the new as a challenge to learn.

C. Acceptance versus dependency (a delicate balance)

"If we walk far enough,' said Dorothy, 'we shall sometime come to some place, I am sure.'" (The Wizard of Oz, 1900).

Dependency is a form of self-destructiveness. It is an innate tendency to resist empowerment. There appears to be a natural, inborn clash of identity between the "I" that is "me" and the "I" that is "we," exclusion versus inclusion. The simultaneous desires to return to the womb (to be totally cared for and to avoid all stress) strongly conflicts with the desire to be in control, to have total power and to be physically and emotionally independent. This struggle creates tension which can be released in constructive or destructive ways. Frequently the way in which we release such tension occurs below our awareness and intent.

To confront or avoid the stress resulting from such discord becomes an issue of competence versus complacency, attempting control or achieving acceptance. As such it is intertwined with the pursuit of progress and contentment. Our self-concept and self-esteem depend upon how we evaluate our ability to satisfy everyday demands while resolving this tension. Do we feel empowered, i.e., reasonably able to successfully overcome most daily challenges? Are we sufficiently forgiving of ourselves for mistakes and shortcomings or are we too easy on ourselves thereby avoiding growth and responsibility and reinforcing the status quo? Are we too reliant on others or do we have the right balance of asking and seeking assistance at the appropriate times?

There is an American Indian saying that; "If I walk alone I travel faster but if I walk with another I travel farther." This is the dilemma that faces all of us and at its heart is accepting what you can't control (and getting help) and changing what you can (settling conflict independently). To achieve our ultimate goals we should avoid both self-destructive dependency needs which can enslave us and the arrogance of self-sufficiency which can isolate us and lead to decline. We should fend off false pride and seek assistance when appropriate. Finding the balance is crucial and complex.

D. Self-acceptance

For Robert Karen, Ph. D, self-acceptance allows an individual to have the confidence "…that he can be all things (good or bad), he is without fear of shame or rejection." It also allows that person "…to grant that freedom to others. It is the cornerstone of the forgiving spirit." (Karen, 2001). Self-acceptance is forgiving others as well as ourselves. Without such acceptance, we blame everyone and view the world as separate and hostile in a self-protective attempt to avoid guilt and shame.

E. Acceptance and judgment

"Dorothy said nothing. Oz had not kept the promise he made her but he had done his best, so she forgave him. As he said, he was a good man, even if he was a bad Wizard."
(The Wizard of Oz, 1900).

The miracle of acceptance is that we do not judge and therefore we have no need to forgive. Acceptance of ourselves, others and circumstances means living our daily lives without having to say "would" "should" or "could." Acceptance is embracing the moment and all the feelings, thoughts and actions occurring at that point in time. It is to embody awareness of the moment and the intent to love. It is to applaud the past which brought us to this place and trust in the future which will be generated from this place. Therefore the goal is to embrace what is and to resist our initial reaction to frame, limit and demean the present by preserving inaccurate memories and perspectives from the past. Acknowledge this moment as an occasion to affirm our life and destiny, to have compassion and to avoid accusation.

To accept and forgive ourselves is to embrace all that is human. It is to see in others kinship and kindness. It is to derive strength and greater self-acceptance from the unity and closeness we feel. Thus through acceptance, a mutually reinforcing cycle develops increasing our spirituality and contentment. "In this realm of positive self-regard, we do not expect ourselves to be perfect. Our limitations are not a cause for self-laceration or despair." (Karen, 2001).

In order to accept ourselves, we must come to the realization that strengths and weaknesses come from the same source and they too, are reciprocal. Each can evolve into the other depending upon the situation at the moment. For example, at different times, our resolve can become our obstinacy, our caring can become controlling, our concern can become intrusive, our gifts can become bribes and our trust can become gullibility.

True self-acceptance is a gift to ourselves and others. It requires the honesty and integrity to face our weaknesses with caring and our strengths with skepticism. It is the ability to perceive ourselves both as we are and as we can be. The result is a more loving and tolerant self.

F. Accepting our past

"Reality is a construction of what we remember."
(Fred Alan Wolf, 2006).

If I am to love myself, I must accept my history. I must reconcile my early memories with today's circumstances because that is what makes me who I am. It serves no purpose to become a victim or a slave to resentment. Blame and regret only reinforce misconceptions and keep you in their throes. Do not allow thoughts of defect, defeat or inability prejudice the memories of the past because they will seep into perspectives of the present.

You are perfectly you and the result of an imperfect life story. If you are content with who you are now, no matter what happened then, no matter how painful or destructive, you got through it. The lessons may have been difficult but they helped shape who you are. You are here, now, and that's exactly where you should be. Extract the gift of growth, gratitude and learning from the past. Past, present and future merge at this moment. It is your responsibility to re-create yourself and fulfill your destiny. You have all you need to be successful right here, right now.

What you must realize and embrace from this is:

1. You are a miracle.

2. Your higher power has put you where you are now for a reason.

3. Your past is exceptional and contributes to your individuality.

4. Your individuality allows you to exclusively contribute to a greater plan.

5. Accepting these ideas will give you the impetus to move forward (rather than remaining in regret) and achieve that which you cannot even imagine.

How you frame and how you view previous events will define and determine your reaction to new events. You can alter the view of the past by changing your current self-concept. In this way, your perspective regarding former circumstances will gradually become more consistent with your present frame of reference and world-view. A revised self-concept will transform behavior which in turn will reshape the world's response to you. Have the courage to begin this journey and free yourself from all negative aspects in your memory.

IV. Summary

"Of all the dangerous energies that can breed inside our minds, one of the most harmful to our contentment is the wish that things were otherwise." (James Hoover, 1977).

Acceptance is one of the four spiritual qualities or attitudes we must cultivate in order to live a peaceful and fulfilled life. It is one of the four spiritual pillars which supports love, wisdom and courage, the primary components of contentment.

The central challenge is to temper pride, anger, jealousy, and greed so that our spiritual path is clear and our focus is on love. As we grow, our goal becomes service, self-awareness and self-discovery. We must learn and appreciate who we are and how we are evolving as we strive to realize our potential. We need to observe thoughts, feelings, and behaviors in different situations and evaluate the consequences of these. We should shed the skin of the past and view each moment and each interaction as a blessed opportunity to learn and change. Each challenge is a chance to learn our identity and our role in life. None of this can begin without the knowledge and awareness that we are made of God's love and are perfectly Her creation.

When we begin to doubt and when we feel alone and abandoned, it is always good to pray. "God give me the grace to embrace my journey. Let me accept my failures without self-condemnation. Let me falter without demeaning my past or blaming my present. Most importantly, let me embrace my successes both small and large while giving thanks for your guidance on this journey of empowerment and self-discovery."

V. For Further Consideration

1. Acceptance is one of the four spiritual qualities that are necessary for love, wisdom, and courage.

2. Love, wisdom and courage are the main components of a contented, fulfilled and empowered life.

3. Acceptance has an active ("to affirm," etc.) and passive ("to go along with") meaning, both of which are relevant for achieving our goal of compassion and contentment.

4. Acceptance is the first spiritual quality requested in The Serenity Prayer.

5. Acceptance leads to empowerment.

6. Acceptance is a quality that requires awareness and intent in each moment.

7. Acceptance is manifested as unconditional love or unconditional positive regard.

8. Self-acceptance is necessary to achieve serenity in all other areas of our lives.

9. In order to attain self-acceptance, we must be diligent in our fight against labels from the past which have demeaned us and others.

10. Acceptance, forgiveness, gratitude, trust and humility are the primary components of love.

11. Acceptance begins with humility and gratitude.

12. Acceptance means empowerment not passivity.

13. Achieving acceptance is hampered by our natural and chronic need to blame, resent and judge.

14. Acceptance is hampered by the consumer culture which defines us as fundamentally deprived, deficient and defective.

15. Acceptance helps us resist the tendency towards dependency because we celebrate our competence.

16. Acceptance means we understand that our strengths and weaknesses come from the same source.

17. We must learn to accept our past because it has created the present for which we are grateful.

Chapter 7

Patience/Trust
The Universe Does Not Work On
Your Schedule

"But it takes time to make a raft, even when one is as industrious and untiring as the Tin Woodman." (The Wizard of Oz, 1900).

I. Definition

The current usage of "patience" implies both an active and passive meaning. It can be passive indicating "an act of waiting without distress or complaint." There is also an active definition in which "patience" denotes "the persistent pursuit of a particular goal despite pain and hardship."

The American Heritage Dictionary defines "patience" as (1) "enduring pain or difficulty with calmness"; (2) "tolerant, understanding"; (3) "persevering"; and (4) "capable of calmly awaiting outcome; not hasty or impulsive." The word "patience" is derived from the Old French and the Latin "patientia" meaning 'to suffer.'

"Trust" is defined by the same source as: "to rely or depend on;" "to have confidence in" and "to believe." "Trust" is derived from Old Norse "traustr" meaning "strong."

II. Patience In Everyday Life

"How poor are they that have not patience? What wound did ever heal but by degrees?" (Othello, Act II, Shakespeare).

A. The general role of patience in achieving contentment

Patience is one of the four pillars and spiritual traits, which supports love, wisdom and courage. It is a compassionate quality which emanates from and yet reinforces humility, gratitude and acceptance in a continual cycle of wellness.

Patience allows us the opportunity to reflect on circumstances and thereby delay gratification and control impulsivity. It serves as a reminder to strive for the wisdom that directs attention to our strengths. Patience gives the pause that helps us ponder what is and what is not in our control. It allows time to gather the courage to act on this knowledge and generate an outcome from which we can learn. In turn, we then progress and more effectively pursue our goals.

Patience expresses and is nurtured by acceptance, love and most importantly a humble trust in a power greater than ourselves, as well as faith in a universal plan. Patience is the caring and nurturant mother, caressing and reassuring the growing child. It is the feeling of security that no matter what frustrates me or spoils my expectations, all will be well if I accept and listen to my feelings and trust in a power greater than myself. There was a West Coast saying in the 1970's that sums this up, "Relax, ride the wave and you'll eventually get to the beach."

B. Patience and harmony

"Patience is the best remedy for every trouble."
Titus Maccius Plantus (254 – 184 BC).

The ability to be patient is the gift of aligning oneself with the natural rhythm of nature as well as the natural rhythm of the self (biorhythms). Rather than indulge in the impulse to act and to take control, a few sacred seconds of thoughtful awareness helps fulfill our Personal Development Program and higher goals.

Most importantly, through patience we resist the action or thought that distracts us in the moment. When feeling frustrated, angry or resentful it is likely that we are overcome by an external event and have lost inner focus. In these situations we need to surrender to contemplation, understanding, empathy and love.

C. Patience and compassion

"First, keep the peace within yourself, then you can also bring peace to others." (Thomas A. Kempis, 1380 – 1471).

Patience helps us listen with our ears and hearts even to those with whom we disagree. Through patience we gain a new understanding and compassion for our fellow travelers. It allows us to cherish the challenge of a new situation because we realize that we have an opportunity to learn and grow. On a more macro level, patience enables us to accept the insanity of the world, as opposed to becoming a participant in that pathology, trusting that at this moment a better situation can be created. Patience is the calm that prevents the storm. It is reassurance and pause during an upheaval. It brings order to chaos and lets our higher power work miracles.

D. Patience can be active or passive

"The Scarecrow, who was never tired, stood up in another corner and waited patiently until morning came."
(*The Wizard of Oz*, 1900).

The meaning of the word "patience" can have an active or passive form. It can mean the passive act of waiting without getting upset or it can mean persisting or intending to persist towards a goal despite many obstacles and impediments. It can be understood as maintaining calm with no action in the face of turmoil or taking a forceful role while attempting to overcome something that prevents or hinders us from achieving our goal. It can be seen as a resignation, based on a belief that we are not in command and that a power far wiser than we, directs events as part of a larger, greater plan. On the other hand, it can mean that we believe we can alter an outcome and achieve our objective if only we don't give up. According to The American Heritage Dictionary "perseverance" means "to persist or remain constant in an idea, task or purpose despite obstacles." Patience generates and nurtures courage, wisdom and humility while managing impulse, irrationality, and irresponsibility.

Patience is intentional decision making. We decide whether or not to take action in a stressful situation. However, we are passive in our view of the outcome. Patience recognizes that the results of our behavior are part of a more encompassing design and the best that we could do given the circumstances. Patience suppresses the "shoulds, coulds or woulds" and evaluates the "now" objectively. It embraces the spirit and suppresses the "child-self's" insistence on wish fulfillment and immediate gratification. Patience gives us the power over time in that we focus on the "now" as we suspend prior anguish and frustration as well as the impulse to immediately react based on existent bias.

F. Patience, persistence and success

"Patience will bring the snail to Jerusalem." (Irish Proverb).

Patience reinforces persistence which is a necessary quality for success. Thomas Edison associated success with patience when in response to a question stated: "I have not failed seven hundred times. I have not failed once. I have succeeded in proving that those seven hundred ways will not work. When I finally have eliminated the ways that will not work, I will find the way that will." This is the gift and the practice of patience.

The writer, Gustave Flanbert said: "talent is long patience." It is persistence, endurance, determination, passion and trust. As we begin to understand that a purpose of any current task may simply be to give us an opportunity to strengthen our frustration tolerance, we will be more able to strategize and succeed. It is a necessary trait for empowerment and contentment because with patience, thought dominates emotion.

G. Patience in the moment

Patience is a function of living in the moment. It is to accept what is placed before you without invoking memories of the past (e.g., "he always does this") or the future (e.g., "if I allow this to continue, I will be doomed, my life will change irrevocably.") Patience is stepping back and allowing sacred seconds to process mental, physical and emotional reactions. It delays response and promotes deliberation thereby mitigating desire and impulse. Patience gives us the strength to be in the moment.

Throughout the day we should practice being in the moment. On a regular basis become aware of all the senses. Focus on the sights, sounds, smells and sensations of your surroundings. When exercising, concentrate on the rhythmic repetitions of your body. Note your thoughts and feelings as you respond to physical changes. This moment, these sensations can never occur again and each day presents you with unique opportunities, challenges and choices. If you practice patience and awareness, you will receive benefits far beyond expectations.

When we intentionally practice patience, we practice awareness, being in the moment, fully feeling and focusing. Similar to meditation it is a discipline of the mind. It embraces the now. It is gratitude, humility and empowerment all in the same soup, served in a exquisite bowl. Patience connects us with the self and the rhythms of nature.

Patience and awareness facilitate learning says M.J. Ryan (2003), "The way to cultivate more patience is to see ourselves as learners and on each occasion of impatience as an opportunity to grow." We create true change by becoming aware of our actions. It is this awareness, being in the moment, which frees us of our shackled past and future fears. Sylvia Boorstein (2002) writes: "We are all dangling in mid-process between what already happened (which is just a memory) and what might happen (which is only an idea). Now is the only time anything happens." Be open to now; don't distort it with the past and don't dismiss it with the future.

H. Summary

We can develop the skill of patience during our everyday routine. Patience gives us the opportunity to pause and reflect thereby increasing awareness of fleeting thoughts and feelings as well as delaying the impulse to immediately react. It helps us become more cognizant of our impressions and our situation. Relationships improve with patience as we become listeners rather than lecturers and as we begin to think of "we" rather than "me."

Everyday we can rehearse being observers rather than managers as we develop patience. When we pause and objectively assess, instead of acting and personalizing, we become more adept at comprehending the entire situation rather than being blinded by our biased and simplistic version of the present.

Additionally, patience can provide the strength to persist in our quest for goodness and contentment. It allows us to learn from experience and to frame the "cup as half full." It enables us to uncover opportunity in missteps and to view the unpredictable as part of a larger, more benevolent plan. Each day patience suppresses judgment and embraces the spirit. Indeed, patience enhances every aspect of our lives and makes the journey towards fulfillment a more sacred and satisfying quest.

III. Patience and Trust

"Patience and trust go hand in hand."
(A Course in Miracles, 1996).

Patience emanates from a trust of the self and its capabilities as well as the goodness, benevolence and wisdom of the universe. Trust is a knowing and a feeling that the universe is benign. "Yes, I am here for a good reason and I have all I need to fulfill my destiny." When things become challenging or they don't concur with our plans, we know that we will be okay and that this crisis is part of a bigger picture. What choice do we have? Is it better to curse the dark? To rant and rave about injustice? To feel like the victim? Or is it better to allow the events that we can't control eventuate and instead focus intently on what we can do to change our reactions, thoughts and feelings?

If we do not personalize, catastrophize and/or externalize, solutions will come faster and be more effective. We then empower ourselves by controlling our responses to the unexpected. Dr. Dyer (1999) writes that: ". . . whatever is supposed to come to your life will be there when you have developed the capacity to receive it." With either expected or unexpected change, we can move toward growth. Either enables us to build our spiritual selves and either one can be met with love and serenity. Most importantly, for this to happen we must develop trust.

Look around you. The world is moving without your help.

Growth is everywhere. Take a suggestion from Dr. Dyer (2001): "By observing nature, your nature and the natural world around you, you will see that you must allow a wound to progress at its own pace; to eat a fig you must first let it flower, put forth fruit and ripen. Trust in your nature and let go of your desire to have things done quickly"…and in your own way.

Trust is believing that we always have just what we need, just when we need it. This is our time, our moment, our opportunity. We must learn to trust our ability to do what is necessary so as to be aligned with destiny. Many dilemmas are caused by a fear which entices us to manage and supervise a stressful situation. Special problems arise when we try to take charge of circumstances which are more powerful than our limited abilities. It is essential that we have sufficient humility and trust to comprehend this so that we allow such events to unfold. Letting go and believing that things will resolve successfully is a way to reach contentment. Believing in the moment and intending love will gradually give us the wisdom to cope with change. When we have faith, we develop the empowerment and confidence to know what can be changed and what must be turned over and let go.

A. <u>Summary</u>

> *"'That's all right,' said the Scarecrow. 'You are quite welcome to take my head off, as long as it will be a better one when you put it on again.'" (<u>The Wizard of Oz</u>, 1900).*

Part of generating gratitude is understanding the type of trust expressed by the Scarecrow. Part of gratitude is understanding that the Universe is generally benign and in fact has provided all we need to achieve our goals. From this awareness spawns a certainty which allows us to perform daily duties with the confidence that we are participating in a marvelous, cosmic dance. Like a small link in a big chain, our role is both crucial and secondary to this larger plan. Patience allows us to trust in the plan and realize that events unfold in God's time and not ours. At first this is alarming and anxiety provoking but as we develop faith we feel a contentment that is unique in our experience. Ultimately we let go, observe, learn and move on, all according to a plan which we can witness and surmise but never dictate. Now we can use the time we wait in line to catch up on our reading or recall our gratitude. During periods of stress, remember that we don't have to be the sheriff for there to be respect and order in our Universe.

IV. The Power of Patience

"Genius is only a greater aptitude for patience."
Comte De Buffon (1707 – 1788).

A. Patience and strength

Patience is sometimes seen as weakness, fear, passivity and/or lack of commitment. In truth, it is quite the opposite. Patience is having the gift of faith and trust. It is a certainty that whatever happens and whenever it happens will be responded to in a way that will appropriately resolve the issue. Patience also reflects an assumption that the universe is benevolent and that our trials and tribulations are simply directional signs toward growth. As John F. Kennedy (1/20/61) said: "Rejoice in hope and be patient in tribulation."

B. Patience produces persistence

"After the Lion had rested they started along the road of yellow brick, silently wondering, each in his own mind, if ever they would come to the end of the woods and reach the bright sunshine again."
(The Wizard of Oz, 1900).

Both Winston Churchill and Thomas Edison knew the value of patience in generating persistence and contributing to success. Success is the ". . . ability to go from one failure to another with no loss of enthusiasm" according to Churchill. Edison wrote that: "Many of life's failures are people who did not realize how close they were to success when they gave up."

Patience reflects the confidence we have in ourselves. It urges us to continue towards our goal in the face of doubt, insecurity and the unknown. It tells us that we are on the right course despite what others may say. Patience is one of the four pillars of contentment. It is a necessary spiritual quality which helps us to fulfill our destiny. Patience is the result of developing humility, gratitude, acceptance, and trust. Empowerment embodies patience and they are reciprocal qualities, they engage in a dance of mutual reinforcement. Patience is self-control and self-possession.

C. <u>Patience propagates pause and reinforces choice</u>

Every moment offers us a choice. This puts us in control of our lives despite fear and resistance. We can become aware of our emotions in the moment. Fear, anger, tension, as well as happiness, love, contentment, etc. are simply amounts of energy going through our body generated by our interpretation of external events.

Patience helps us pause and access the knowledge we need to develop a strategy to resolve strain caused by circumstances and emotional reactions. Patience tells us to slow down, don't immediately respond. This split second, this nanosecond allows our love to become part of the resolution. Patience says: "Wait" while the child-self says "take over and act." Patience is the sacred pause; the breaks in the engine of impulsiveness and the destination of trust and acceptance. For M.J. Ryan (2003), patience is an integral part of our well being and she recommends that we practice patience in order to cope and grow in love and wisdom.

Patience reflects self-control and self-discipline. External affronts ultimately have little to do with our internal state.

It's our choice. We are in control. The four horsemen of self-destructiveness; impulsivity, envy, aggression and frustration are effectively neutralized when we practice patience and deliberation. Patience encourages us to enjoy life and accept the hand dealt us. Patience says that it is more important to delay gratification than to succumb to the desire for immediate relief. Patience supplies the courage to tolerate fear and to trust in the unknown.

As a final point, we must accept the idea that the venture is as important as the destination. If we are to make the most of our quest, to fully realize and experience it, we must grow from our missteps and miscues. During times of frustration, introspection allows us to step back, learn and regenerate. All are functions of patience.

Frustration is caused by magnifying the importance of a particular moment to the detriment and minimalization of the overall picture. The attitude that "this too will pass" serves us well in maintaining a balanced perspective and persistence towards our goal. Like acceptance; "Patience is the willingness to be in the now exactly as it is." (Ryan, 2003). Patience is one more spiritual characteristic that we must foster if we are to achieve contentment.

D. <u>Patience and self-respect</u>

Patience is both a cause and an effect of self-respect and self-acceptance. Patience is antithetical to the self-absorbed mind set which can be so destructive to ourselves and our relationships. As we get out of our own way, patience allows life to unfold without meddling. We let go and let God as the 12 step programs recommend. It gives us the capacity to step back, to learn and to cherish the moment.

In The Power of Patience (2003), M.J. Ryan writes: "Patience in the form of acceptance allows us to have empathy for others because we recognize as human beings we all have limitations. It gives us the emotional resilience to respond with kindness, to feel compassion." "Through this acceptance of others as they are and life as it is in this moment we prove our true strength."

Anger is the result of deficient respect and empathy. It is the expression of our child self wanting things one way, absolutely and immediately. It is based on the fear of losing control over the external, the fear of trusting in a plan greater than our own. Anger is an attempt through physical means to regain power. Expressing anger inappropriately negates self-respect and generates attempts at self-justification. Isn't it ironic that we lose internal control to gain (we hope) external control?

E. Patience as part of our life's mission

Don't give up in your quest to develop patience. You are on a mission which no one else can accomplish. Ask for and you will receive all the spiritual help and encouragement you need to successfully complete that mission. Be focused, be determined and succeed. Reflect and expand the will of the spirit.

F. Summary – the power of patience

Patience, humility, gratitude and acceptance are assets in our quest for growth and fulfillment. While it is frequently seen as a weakness in our culture, in actuality, patience arises from a deep certainty of the self that all stress, crises, and conflicts can and will be resolved. Patience promotes success because it generates persistence. In turn, persistence is born of trust in ourselves and our higher power. Despite doubt, insecurity and the unknown, persistence keeps us focused and motivated.

Patience enhances awareness of the moment and counteracts the tendency to immediately react to unpleasant emotions. It promotes pause and reflection allowing us to put an event in perspective. We become able to exercise our power to choose and therefore strengthen integrity and self-esteem. Patience reminds us that we are in control and that ultimate power resides within us not outside us. We make more effective and loving decisions when we have patience.

Because patience helps us control our child-self, it bolsters and fortifies self-respect and empathy. Consequently, we can more readily accept others and their defects. We begin to view those who most annoy as giving us an opportunity to grow. In sum, patience is a spiritual and mental trait that will improve every aspect of our lives and help us fulfill our ultimate mission.

V. Impediments to Patience

"Patience is needed with everyone but most of all ourselves."
(St. Francis de Sales).

Throughout life, the child-self in its destructive capacity, collides with the positive forces of growth to save the status quo. It seeks to keep us dormant and to retain the fictitious security of bygone days. The child-self is very clever and insidious. We must constantly be aware of its presence, especially in the forms of apathy and paralysis, victimization and rationalization.

A. Patience and projection

Projection for the purpose of this discussion means to imagine all of the possible, negative outcomes, if one takes a particular action right now. It has the potential to be a significant barrier to persistence and patience because many painful memories of unintended consequences become conscious, causing anxiety and preventing advancement. The great "what if . . . ?" is entertained, fueling an expectation of doom and failure. The child-self gains strength as it interrupts development and maturation.

This is a familiar bind and is often the cause of perniciously pursuing the same strategy, hoping to render different results. We embrace the familiar to avoid the anxiety of assertiveness and the repercussions of the unknown. The thought that: "the devil you know is better than the devil you don't" arises and we now can contentedly rely on the premise that doing nothing is the best thing. All's well and "if it ain't broke don't fix it." But it is broken and it needs to be fixed. Patience and trust will motivate us to begin such a vast journey with a small step. Patience, courage, and trust will quell the voice of the child-self and allow the spiritual voice of growth and fulfillment to resound.

Mark Twain once said: "The worst troubles I've had in my life are the one's that never happened." This is the essence of projection. This is the core of the self-destructive tendency to do nothing rather than something, to stay the course rather than altering that course and to bask in the familiar as we close our eyes to future promise and accomplishment. If we are to achieve contentment we must move forward, risk and change our behavior.

B. <u>Patience and reproachful judgment</u>

"Patience is the companion of wisdom."
(St. Augustine 354-430 AD).

Patience and reproachful judgment cannot coexist. In the moment, we can chose to have one or the other. Impatience is a judgment. It is a disease of the "shoulds." "He should know better." "This should not be happening" (a.k.a. "This is not fair"). "Life should be different," etc. Get over it!! It is what it is; they are who they are and no amount of whining, wishing or wailing is going to change that.

Patience is trust and acceptance. Criticism nullifies these as the child-self strives to regain control and savor superiority. Faultfinding attempts to mitigate the unpleasant feeling of vulnerability by assigning blame and responsibility to others. Patience is antithetical to judgment because it is a confidence begotten by a belief that we are blessed and all will be well. When challenge comes, patience allows us to persist and endure because we reason instead of judging, listen instead of rebuking. We know that the flower will bloom, the wind will blow and people will be people. It's all good and patience allows us to accept that.

C. **Patience and our culture of immediate gratification**

"Getting it now takes too long." (A child overhead at a local mall).

Again culture militates against serenity and maturation. It caters to our child-self insisting that all good things come at once and waiting is the equivalent of rejection. We erroneously maintain that if we are loved we must have our wants met immediately. The distinction between needs and desires is purposely blurred and consumerism creates a constant sense of urgency, dissatisfaction and deprivation.

Patience leads to contentment because we understand that one desire will soon be replaced by another and it's all for naught, resulting in emptiness and frustration. True satisfaction and contentment only come with the realization that in the here and now we have all we will ever need. Everything else is a bonus, the proverbial cherry atop the cake.

Humility begets gratitude which in turn begets patience and acceptance. Now we can be in the moment, to witness our reactions and to judge their validity. How many times do we say "Do I really need this?" Listen to your inner wisdom. Enjoy the fullness of the universe in yourself and give thanks, not cash. Treasure what is and you won't need to purchase what might be.

We have to lose the arrogance of self-importance: the illogic of "if I want it, I must need it and I must have it now because I deserve it" or "I'm that important and life owes this to me", needs to stop. Thoughts such as these suppress our true loving nature and transform us into consumption machines. We are no longer people, we are automatons of acquisition. We are what we have and if we don't have it, we are nothing. How sad!

D. Patience and fear

"All things come round to him who will but wait."
(Henry Wadsworth Longfellow, 1857).

Fear significantly impedes the cultivation of patience. Patience needs trust. If we cannot trust ourselves to decrease stress and if we don't trust in the universe for fulfillment and satisfaction, we will easily become irritable, intolerant and impetuous.

Impatience arises when we feel immobilized, vulnerable and powerless. It originates from beliefs like we cannot complete a task on time (e.g., "I'll never get this done in time for . . .") or that something is beyond our ability (e.g., "this is too much, I could never do this . . ."). Usually, the illogical child-self also chimes in with something like: "You'll be doomed, if you don't succeed." During these intervals, patience regains composure by dissecting the task into smaller, more manageable pieces and focusing on what we can control and complete. While we improve, we begin to gain confidence in our ability to cope with surprise and stress. When we pinpoint the positive, past successes rather than past failures are recalled. The child-self's tendency to catastrophize ("We're damned") subsides and the competent parent asserts itself. We develop tools and strategies for the unexpected and over time we realize their effectiveness and our efficiency. As this happens, fear, self-doubt and self-hate diminish.

Ultimately, patience reinforces acceptance, such that we begin to tolerate those people, places, and things that without patience would cause us stress, anger and anxiety. The issue is to reframe (change our perspective) inner stress so that we do not allow it to cloud judgment and influence behavior. In essence, we cope with and neutralize fear by interpreting the situation differently.

As M.J. Ryan says in The Power of Patience (2003), "Patience accomplishes this magic by bringing together three essential qualities of mind and heart that allow us to be and do our best; persistence, serenity and acceptance." With patience we are able to quell inner turmoil and trust in the capacity to overcome any obstacle that confronts us. With patience we develop the skill of accepting what we can't control. We trust that all events which we encounter are part of a plan greater than ourselves and our ability to understand. With this realization, all momentary fear will vanish and serenity will reign.

V. Summary

Patience is one of the four essential spiritual and mental traits (pillars) that both reinforces and is reinforced by growth and contentment. Similar to the other traits, there are internal and external impediments to acquiring and expanding patience in our life.

One such internal impediment is the child-self demanding that every desire is a need and must be instantly gratified or we are eternally unloved, unprotected and unsatisfied. Such beliefs and behaviors prevent patience from progressing and keep us static and frustrated.

The child-self is also reinforced by the consumer culture which rewards dependency and superficiality. Just like an infant distracted by a toy, we look to the outside to avoid the internal drive for maturation and advancement. The consumer culture champions such perspectives while dismissing and discrediting independence, integrity and introspection. Patience mitigates these pressures and promotes progression. It reduces fear and allows us to move forward.

Patience expresses itself actively by persevering towards a goal despite physical, emotional and social barriers. Patience is also expressed passively when we don't act in spite of the child-self demanding immediate gratification. Both expressions of patience are necessary if we are to succeed in all challenges yet each is hampered by feelings and thoughts which subtly lure us into inaction as they sabotage our initial efforts.

VI. For Further Consideration

1. Patience is one of the four pillars of contentment promoting and supporting love, courage and wisdom.

2. Patience can be expressed actively in the form of perseverance or passively in the form of enduring and not acting.

3. Both expressions of patience are necessary to achieve the goals of growth and contentment.

4. Patience promotes awareness of ourselves and our surroundings.

5. Patience impedes impulsive actions and therefore enhances self-respect and self-esteem by allowing intentions of love and compassion to dominate our perspective.

6. As we develop patience we also develop empathy, compassion and acceptance of others. The "I" slowly evolves into the "We."

7. Patience and trust both generate and reinforce the other.

8. Patience is the ultimate strength and it gives rise to persistence, a necessary characteristic for success.

9. Like all qualities that promote growth and contentment, we have a natural resistance to patience and a desire to preserve the status quo.

10. Impulsivity, judging, catastrophizing, anxiety, fear and various other expressions of the child-self attempt to stifle patience and progression in an insidious and insistent manner.

11. Ultimately, patience fosters acceptance which is a direct route to love, wisdom and courage.

Part III

Obstacles and Opportunities

"The sides were so steep that none of them could climb down, and for a moment it seemed that their journey must end."
(*The Wizard of Oz*, 1900).

Judgments and Relationships

"But it is a long way to the Emerald City, and it will take you many days. The country here is rich and pleasant, but you must pass through rough and dangerous places before you reach the end of your journey."

"This worried Dorothy a little, but she knew that only the great Oz could help her get to Kansas again, so she bravely resolved not to turn back." (The Wizard of Oz, 1900).

A Winding Road

Similar to Dorothy, we will encounter encumbrances that will vary in severity and complexity, throughout our journey. However, behind each obstacle there tends to be an opportunity. The most difficult and insidious hurdles are those that are ingrained in the culture and slowly insinuated into our psyche so that they are almost unrecognizable. Comparing and judging others is just such a trait. Contrariwise, relationships, whether intimate or casual, are significant opportunities to learn about ourselves and practice kindness and compassion.

Each day with each interaction we are presented with both obstacles and opportunities to either grow or regress. Judging and comparing is a perfidious habit strongly reinforced by our culture. To judge and compare is a choice we make which functions to exclude and differentiate other individuals or groups. It prevents us from introspection and maturation, substituting a cloak of superiority for honest self-assessment.

Relationships provide us with the occasion to behave differently; to learn and to grow through interaction with another. Judgment and comparison will quickly destroy a relationship while acceptance/forgiveness, patience/trust, humility and gratitude will facilitate the development of all relationships. Furthermore, these are the qualities that constitute love and wisdom and they are the qualities we need to express every day if we are to achieve contentment.

Dorothy is a perfect example of a person who accepts and tries to understand rather than judge. She takes little notice of the oddities or absurd stories of the Lion, Tin Man, or Scarecrow but instead joins with them in their quest for self-improvement. Each has what they are seeking but is blind to this. Rather, they seek outside validation and resolution. With Dorothy's help and their mutual cooperation each overcomes significant barriers to reach the goals of empowerment and self-actualization.

Chapter 8

Judging and Comparing
The Primary Obstacles to
Contentment

"Judge me not, that ye be not judged." (Matthew 7:1).

"Whose house is of glass, must not throw stones at another."
(George Herbert 1593 – 1633).

I. Statement of the Problem

As human beings, we constantly exhibit a need, bordering on a compulsion, to judge, compare and contrast ourselves with others. We yearn to exclude. We wish to feel noteworthy, outstanding, "above the crowd." We aspire to be recognized and acknowledged as separate and distinct. Yet, there is a simultaneous need to merge, to identify with and to eschew isolation by being a part of something considered a secure association. These urges to connect or to isolate naturally conflict yet unfold in all our interactions. How we approach and manage this struggle plays a significant role in maturation as well as whether or not we achieve contentment.

Once again, early upbringing imparts rules as to what is acceptable, discourteous, loving or aggressive. We are also aware of other parameters, especially items communicated by the culture, every minute of every day. Some, such as those instilled in early childhood are hidden by time while many from society are immediate and unrelenting. In either case we scan the behavior of people especially in new situations, to determine if they are friend or foe, in agreement or disagreement, part of the "we" or part of the "them."

Individuals are predisposed to react to these messages differently. It is generally conceded that depressed individuals are internally oriented and judge themselves more often and more harshly than those without depression. They also tend to judge others as stronger than themselves. On the other end of the spectrum, a psychopathic individual is externally oriented and has little inclination for self-blame, viewing the world as a force which causes misery, thereby justifying a destructive retaliation.

The parameters we use to judge ourselves and others are obvious and explicit if culturally ingrained. They are more implicit if the indoctrination occurred earlier in life. Therefore, whether we are internally or externally oriented, we judge, evaluate and test ourselves and others throughout the course of the day. As a result we may feel that we are loved and competent or that we are hated, isolated and inadequate.

A. Judgment and contentment – a natural conflict

"The strain of constant judgment is virtually intolerable. It is curious that an ability so debilitating would be so deeply cherished."
(A Course in Miracles, 1976).

Some things are certain. Judgment and acceptance naturally conflict. Furthermore, both play an integral part in the quality of our lives, how we evolve and our level of satisfaction. The rules by which we judge ourselves and others can be changed, resulting in a marked difference in our emotional well-being, style of interacting and expectations of how we should be treated and how we should treat others.

To achieve a change in this facet of our lives we must remember that judgment/comparison and acceptance/inclusion are polar opposites. You cannot cultivate acceptance while you practice judgment. They are mutually exclusive, oil and vinegar, water and sand. However, they are controlled by our thoughts and choices. We can determine how to view a situation and we can decide how to react to that point of view. Both have consequences that set us on a path of isolation, suspicion and vulnerability or inclusion, trust and competence.

II. Origin of the Problem

"The past is a lighthouse, not a harbor." (Anonymous).

We are taught that we are good or evil, competent or ineffective by caregivers and the culture. As we grow and develop relationships outside the family, we can choose to teach others how we are to be treated or we can be dominated as we were in childhood. All initial lessons come from the outside and to mature we must begin to separate this imposed internal judge from the internal judge of our experience who is more consistent with our true nature. The latter is the self-judge which we must nurture and cultivate so that we further our advancement in love and compassion. No matter where our current perspective is situated, from fear, exclusion, and self-hate to confidence, inclusion and self-love, we must begin to discover who we are and to contradict the self-deprecatory statements which have no basis in our new reality. Since birth parents, church, state, etc., have dictated rules we must digest in order to survive and to become contributing members of society. Such rules decree who we are and who we are not. Are we attractive, loveable, competent or ugly, detestable and clutzy? Now is the time to articulate and challenge the negative concepts, as well as to accentuate and embrace the positive.

A. <u>Concept of Sin</u>

> *"We have surely lost our way."*
> *(Scarecrow, <u>The Wizard of Oz</u>, 1900).*

We are taught about sin. We are taught what we should do in order to fit into society and we are taught that some natural impulses need to be curbed for the greater good. However, when we relate only to the offensive impulses, we run the risk of seeing ourselves as naturally and immutably "evil." We believe that we are defective and deficient because this is what we were taught. In order to defend ourselves against these feelings of weakness and immorality, we begin to see our "evil" in others and the world then becomes a threatening place.

B. <u>Culture and self-loathing</u>

> *"'Aren't they beautiful?' the girl asked, as she breathed in the spicy scent of the flowers.*

> *'I suppose so,' answered the Scarecrow. 'When I have brains I shall probably like them better.'" (<u>The Wizard of Oz</u>, 1900).*

Institutionalized religion labels anti-social tendencies as sin and we learn that to sin is evil and if we sin we are evil. In truth, sin is an anomaly. Sin is that which threatens spiritual, societal and mental health. Vice need not be part of our true nature. It is the domination of impulse over rationality. It is the triumph of the immediate over the delayed, the destructive over the constructive, excess over moderation. It is the conquest of the ego over the spiritual, self interest over love, singularity over unity and connectedness. Literally translated "sin" means "off the mark."

Sin is an institutional and cultural concept that labels certain conduct as wrong and certain people as "sinners" because they violate social norms and "moral" principles. In fact, "sin" can also be viewed usefully as behavior which is self-destructive and/ or destructive to the community. It does not necessarily have to be a condemnation of those who commit such acts. It can be seen as a gauge of spiritual and mental health. The hazard is when we begin to judge ourselves and others as evil as opposed to fallible. When we begin to use this concept to hate ourselves, to separate one group from another or to see one congregation as superior to another, we begin to exclude, to judge and to condemn rather than embrace, understand and accept. This is the pitfall that we must avoid and the major threat endemic in judging and comparing. To seek patience and compassion is to mitigate these injurious effects. Ultimately, the ideal is to balance self-acceptance with self-restraint and self-policing. Be neither harsh nor complacent and look to the ideal while accepting what is in the moment. We can improve by being aware of our faults as we embrace our virtues.

III. Persistence of the Problem

"It is within our power not to make a judgment about something, and so not to disturb our minds . . ." (Marcus Aurelius, 165 CE).

A. The need to judge

Frequently judgment and comparison originate in the desire to counter feelings of depravity arising from "sin" and "improper" behavior. We then judge others to feel respectable if not morally superior. We try to mitigate guilt by thinking "at least I'm not as bad as Fred or Erma, etc.; they . . ." (you fill in the blanks). How many times have we seen another and said to ourselves; "Well, at least I'm not that fat" or "skinny" or "stupid" etc., etc. We constantly judge ourselves and others to determine if we are living up to the standards required by our life story. When we feel bad we tend to look outward to see if someone shares our sins. However, if we accept ourselves and stop judging or comparing, we will no longer need to condemn anyone. We can indeed "live and let live."

When you label, judge or compare you start to generate a separation between yourself and another. Therefore you begin to isolate and exclude. This naturally creates feelings of vulnerability and aggressiveness. It becomes "me" versus "thee." To resolve this it is important to cultivate your sense of connection rather than looking for reasons to reject. To achieve growth and contentment, it is important that we control the propensity to see others as enemies, rivals or sinners. "Our feelings of contentment are strongly influenced by our tendency to compare." (Dalai Lama, 1998).

Judging someone does not define them it defines you. Judging yourself through the eyes of others or allowing others to judge you leads to defensiveness and anger. "As you give so it shall be given to you. If you give with judgment, limitation and stinginess that is what you will create in your life, judgment, limitations, and stinginess." (Zukov, 1999).

B. The importance of developing into the participant/observer

". . . as long as I know myself to be a coward I shall be unhappy."
(Lion, The Wizard of Oz, 1900).

"Nobody can hurt me without my permission."
(Mahatma Gandhi, 1897).

By developing the skill of assessing ourselves objectively and creating a mental barrier or cushion, we become participant/ observers and more content with all aspects of life. We will achieve compassion and empathy as anger subsides and humility ascends. By accepting life in general and those we encounter in particular, we will no longer control or judge, we will simply be and allow others the same freedom. We will be the person who watches the event without becoming the event and cease to put a great deal of emotional energy into that which we can't control. Instead we will focus on ourselves and our reactions to the moment. This will moderate the ill effects of judging and comparing.

C. <u>Guilt as a denial of self-acceptance and vulnerability</u>

"'I will go with you; but I'm too much of a coward to kill the Witch,' said the Lion.'" (The Wizard of Oz, 1900).

Scrupulous self-examination with all of the attendant guilt and recrimination serves no purpose other than immobilizing us, unless we correct the behavior or express remorse. Baseless blame about situations over which we have no control originates in our refusal to accept the fact that we are helpless in many settings. The vulnerability which accompanies this thought fills us with fear and dread. Due to lack of trust and acceptance, we would rather see ourselves responsible than tolerate these stinging sensations. Ultimately, we must concede the concept that a majority of the injuries and injustices impacting on our daily lives are mishaps (and occasions to learn) which cannot be prevented despite the loving intent of ourselves and others and must be endured as they are. We can maximize the results of such situations by objectively reviewing our behavior and the rationale existing at that time. Misguided guilt is a pretense to be more powerful than we are. It is based on fear and the arrogance which is generated by fear. While we must acknowledge errors and correct missteps, guilt is destructive to moral development and mature behavior if it prevents us from making amends and moving forward after misjudgments.

D. <u>Honesty is still the best policy</u>

"The world we see reflects the people we've become and if we do not like what we see in the world, we must face what we don't like within ourselves." (Marianne Williamson, 2004).

Your responsibility if you are to develop is to look at yourself as honestly as possible in the moment. Shed your preconceptions and see things as they are. Your aspirations are part of your persona. It is God's plan. If you conclude that your impulses are destructive to yourself or others then you are not in harmony with the messages of the true self. Somehow you are "missing the mark" and you are on the wrong path. Reconsider the situation and review your thoughts from a loving, inclusive and accepting context. In doing this, you will discover the correct path of action and eliminate the negativity caused in that moment. Be aware of such destructive thoughts and create patience to quell negative impulses and to promote positive results.

E. <u>The blame game</u>

"The more you judge, the less you love."
(Honore De Balzac, 1839).

When we blame others for our discomforts, mistakes, or poor fortune we undermine ourselves and our problem solving potential. Refusing responsibility for a situation comes at a steep cost to growth and contentment. We make ourselves victims instead of becoming empowered and controlling our destiny.

When we perceive power as external, we begin to form hierarchies, judging people by the frivolous and superficial, such as possessions, popularity, social influence, etc. We cease assuming that all living things have intrinsic worth and that they deserve respect simply because they exist. Instead we begin to suppose that the most valued people hold the greatest power and are therefore the most desirable. Those at the bottom of the hierarchy are the extremely vulnerable and least powerful. Therefore, they are the lowest esteemed of our brethren. As such we learn to create classes, discriminate and rate people according to arbitrary rules. Hence, we justify mistreatment and abuse by dehumanizing an entire class or group of people.

Don't blame yourself, others, your past, your present, etc., for current unpleasant conditions. Accept responsibility and be as honest as possible. This is the path to progress, control and serenity. When you blame outside factors for a misfortune, you immediately surrender the power of choice and reason, you then become weak and vulnerable. Although you cannot control many of the events in life, you must learn to master the emotional and behavioral reactions to these events. By accepting and managing what you can, you eliminate self-hate, guilt and vulnerability as you move forward and develop. Never blame others in order to defend and justify yourself.

Blame is one of the ways we sabotage acceptance. We do not take responsibility for misdeeds and therefore attempt to avoid feeling the shame and guilt that accompanies such circumstances. In order to expand, acknowledge and reconcile these feelings with your self-concept and the beliefs about the extent of your control. Blame is an obstacle to forgiveness, unity and the approval of self as well as others. It is therefore extremely self-destructive.

Rather than batter ourselves or blame everyone, we can learn, prevail and progress. Whether it be exercising, taking a class or some other proactive behavior to resist the temptations of self-indulgence and self-pity, we need to establish self-supremacy and become creators of our fate. All humankind shares weaknesses and problems but this is not who we are. There is no need to compare, judge or condemn.

IV. Achieving Resolution

"'If this road goes in, it must come out,' said the Scarecrow, 'and as the Emerald City is at the other end of the road, we must go wherever it leads us.'" (The Wizard of Oz, 1900).

To judge or compare is to separate and exclude. If we are to mature and to achieve both mastery and contentment we need to have compassion and understanding. We ought to include others and embrace ourselves as part of a whole. This is our mission. When we contribute to life, we will develop a more favorable opinion of ourselves, thereby eliminating the need for guilt, blame and self-deprecation.

A. The importance of acceptance

"There is no good in arguing with the inevitable. The only argument available with an east wind is to put on our overcoat." (James Russell Lowell, 1819-1891).

How can we do this? The solution is at once simple yet challenging. The first step is to embrace yourself and your world. The twelve step programs speak of accepting and coping with life "on life's terms." Self-approval will lead to approval of others. For this we need to develop humility, compassion, and empathy. Neither we nor others are inherently evil. We struggle, we learn, and we move on. There are more similarities than differences among us and we must shed past fears and preconceptions about ourselves, others and the world. Endure and confront vulnerability with trust as you grow with love.

While you advance in this process, it's important not to fall into the trap of comparing yourself to others in any way. You are perfectly you and you are unique. There is no one who can offer to others what you can. No one has had the teachers, the experiences, the inborn temperament, the DNA, etc., that you have. Therefore, no one else can have an effect on the moment like you. With each reaction, you can choose whether that effect will be loving or rejecting. The results of this choice are yours and determine your progress.

B. The role of humility

"I am Dorothy, the Small and Meek. I have come to you for help."
(The Wizard of Oz, 1900).

In heeding the Serenity Prayer and developing acceptance, courage and wisdom, we acknowledge the importance of humility. To be truly humble is to accept our place in the Universe as one part of an infinitely complex and beneficent plan. We have a responsibility to make a contribution to this plan by achieving our potential. As humble individuals we recognize and embrace this. We understand that each event is an opportunity to express individuality, to learn, improve and most importantly to love. With humility, we begin to comprehend that we cannot complete this task alone. From this flows prayer.

C. Service

"'That's all right,' said the Stork, who was flying beside them. 'I always like to help anyone in trouble.'" (The Wizard of Oz, 1900).

"May I be a torch for those in need of light, a bed for those in need of a bed, and a servant for those in need of service."
(Shantideva, 7th century C.E.).

How can we manifest the principles of the four pillars in our lives, so that we may attain contentment and tranquility? The answer given by philosophers and spiritual leaders throughout the centuries is service to others. Ask not what the universe can do for you, rather ask: "How may I serve?" Devotion to the well-being of another and random acts of kindness enable us to realize our true selves and to attain the serenity which accompanies this. A wave, a friendly hello, practicing respect and kindness every day is key. When greeting others, Hindus and Buddhists use the word "Namaste" which loosely means "I honor the place where you and I are one." As we begin to serve others we will become ". . . less judgmental and more forgiving. You will begin seeing that judging others doesn't define them as much as you." (Dyer, 2001).

Small changes result in more dynamic movement creating a critical mass and generating mutual growth. "Nobody made a greater mistake than he who did nothing because he could only do a little." (Edmund Burke, 1775 CE). Every act of kindness and love makes a difference no matter how insignificant it may seem at the time. To pick a rose is to move a star and to hold a hand in need is to embrace heaven.

D. Say "good-bye" to regret

Through these actions we will achieve freedom, fulfillment and self-satisfaction. If we are content with who we are in the moment, it becomes impossible and illogical to be bitter about the past or to harbor resentments. Understand and recognize that it is the very past which we curse that has resulted in the blessings of the moment. Develop gratitude for what you have and who you have become. Shed desire for what you think you need or what "should" be. Look around you and be grateful.

The fact is that your higher power has given you everything while the consumer culture tells you all you lack. As M.J. Ryan writes in Happiness Makeover (2005): "If you find yourself in deep regret over choices we made long ago, remember that the story you are telling yourself about what marvelous things would have come to pass if you'd only made another choice, is just that, a story. In reality, you have no idea where that choice would have led."

Now, you have the keys to release your mind from the prison of remorse. The past is done, the future is yet to be but for today you can control thoughts, feelings and behavior as you become aware of new possibilities and focus intent on humbly beginning your journey of service. Regrets are chains to the status quo. As you rejoice in the moment, bitterness will disappear, replaced by gladness. Dr. Wayne Dyer emphasizes this in all of his work.

"At this point, hopefully, you will begin to forgive yourself. This is the first step to forgiving others. You will see mistakes as lessons for you to transcend. This will free you from the tyranny of self-recrimination." (Dyer, 2001). In terms of self-judgment Dr. Dyer writes that you, "…cannot fail at anything. Everything you do or don't do produces a result. It is what you do with the results that count."

E. Seeking the good

> "To overcome evil with good is good; to overcome evil with evil is evil. (Muhammad, 570-632 CE).

What is "good" or "not good" is an issue both of morality and of mental health. Doing "good" for its own sake means that we do not seek a tangible reward of objects, opinions or praise when we behave in a loving, compassionate manner. Rather, good deeds should be voluntary actions intended only to help another. As such, they will result in growth and gratification. Therefore, every situation in which we suspend judgment and ask "how can I serve?" or "how can I respond with love?" will promote satisfaction and well-being.

V. Summary

> "Instead of comparing our lot with that of those who are more fortunate, we should compare it with the lot of the great majority of our fellow men." (Helen Keller, 1952).

In order to achieve enrichment and serenity, we must shed self-destructive beliefs generated from our past. Among them is the belief that we are defective, sinful and basically corrupt. We are not evil and we were not born evil. God doesn't make mistakes. Because things don't go your way does not mean you failed. Learn to allow things to be other than what you want or feel you need. Accept what is. Events are neither good nor bad, so suspend judgment and comparison. The universe is not focused on us, rather we are a very small but significant part of a life force that is far beyond anything we can imagine or understand.

Life is not a journey of judgment, it is a process of discovery, a mission to express love and unity. Part of this process is to attain acceptance of self and others. Judgment is not ours to render. Comparison is fruitless because we are all uniquely gifted; we all contribute to the grand plan in our own significant way. Our goal is to cherish who we are, to accept others and to understand the importance of sharing this belief. People are no longer rivals or threats. They are fellow travelers on the same journey.

We have to embrace our unity, mission, humanity and common destination. We need to allow ourselves to be greater than self-imposed limits. Success is not more toys and possessions. Success is service and sharing. Dare to risk being kind for no other reason than to express love and compassion.

VI. For Further Consideration

"The most sublime act is to set another before you."
(William Blake, 1757-1827).

1. One of our earliest lessons is who, what and how to judge and compare.

2. Judgment by its nature either includes or excludes.

3. The need for union with others conflicts frequently with the need to judge.

4. Harsh judgment of the self can lead to low self-esteem and depression.

5. Harsh judgment of another can lead to exclusion, aggression, fear and hatred.

6. Acceptance will mitigate the destructive and painful feelings generated by judgment and comparison.

7. Acceptance of self precedes acceptance of others.

8. Acceptance will lead to compassion, empathy and love which in turn will create contentment and growth.

9. A destructive way to cope with the untoward feelings generated by guilt is to bitterly judge and arrogantly compare ourselves with others.

10. Frequently the purpose of guilt is to reinforce the delusion of power and control thereby mitigating feelings of helplessness and vulnerability.

11. The Serenity Prayer is an excellent tool to refocus on what we do and don't control.

12. A fundamental goal is to trust in our higher power and to accept that which we can't control and is not destructive.

13. We must articulate the preconceptions we have of ourselves, others and the world through honest introspection. We can then evaluate them and determine their positive or negatives effects on advancement.

14. Avoid blame and take responsibility for all that you can control.

15. Blame and victimhood weaken and disempower you.

16. Remember that you may not be able to effect much that goes on around you but you can regulate your reactions to and interpretations of circumstances.

17. Always seek love and inclusion by approaching new situations with compassion and empathy.

18. Service to others is a key component to living a life of gratitude and fulfillment.

19. If you are generally content with who you are and your current circumstances, it is illogical that you would harbor resentments and grudges about the past.

20. Don't judge and compare the past ("would," "should," "could"); rather live in the present with love and acceptance. The future will benignly unfold as it was meant to.

Chapter 9

Relationships – The Key to Self Knowledge

"To be emotionally committed to somebody is very difficult, but to be alone is impossible." (Stephen Sondheim).

"It was Toto that made Dorothy laugh, and saved her from growing as grey as her other surroundings." (The Wizard of Oz, 1900).

I. Definition and General Background

According to The American Heritage Dictionary (4th edition, 2001), relationship is: 1) A logical or natural association between two or more things. 2) The connection of people by blood or marriage. "Relations" are defined as: "mutual dealings or connections, as among persons, groups or nations."

A. <u>Origins</u>

> *"'I might have stood there always if you had not come along,'*
> *he said; 'so you have certainly saved my life.'"*
> *(Scarecrow, <u>The Wizard of Oz</u>, 1900).*

In our daily lives as we respond to that which is around us based on our history and concomitant self concept, we often look to other people to fix us, to ease our pain, to make us feel secure and valuable. In essence we look to others to find ourselves. Often, when we fear vulnerability, and cannot trust, relationships become about acquisition, similar to a trip to the mall. Companions, friends and colleagues become extensions of ourselves to supplement an emptiness which cannot be filled. They become objects to consume and control.

As with anything external, such relationships will not cure the internal. Desolation and anxiety remain, we cling, control and manipulate but to no avail. Marianne Williamson (1992) writes: "When we look to another to complete us, we doom the relationship because we are subconsciously looking to it to be what it is not." Yet, in an ideal situation, relationships become the key to contentment and self-knowledge. Patience, trust, acceptance, humility and gratitude are among the necessary qualities which must be cultivated so that relationships become the tools of growth that they were intended to be.

B. <u>Relationships, intimacy and spirituality</u>

In Indian yoga human relationships are viewed as arenas for spiritual practice, classrooms for the sacred. According to Lama Surya Das (<u>The Big Questions</u>, 2007), the word "yoga" actually means union or reunion. "It has a similar derivation etymologically as the word 'religion' which means to unite or rejoin."

For psychologist John Bowlby (1969), "...intimate attachments to other human beings are the hub around which a person's life revolves. From these intimate attachments a person draws strength and enjoyment of life and through what he contributes, he gives strength and enjoyment to others. These are matters about which science and traditional wisdom are one."

C. Intimacy and mental health

"But, alas! I had no heart, so that I lost my love for the Munchkin girl, and did not care whether I married her or not."
(Tin Man, The Wizard of Oz, 1900).

Bowlby believed that separation from others and interpersonal loss are at the very roots of fear, sadness and sorrow. For Dr. Erich Fromm (1941), another psychologist, the most basic fear of all humankind was to be separated from others. The experience of separateness which was first encountered at birth was the source of all anxiety according to Fromm.

Intimacy and competent interpersonal relations are crucial to maintaining sound emotional health. To love, to play, to plan and to work are the goals we achieve when we function as mentally healthy individuals. Intimacy is not dependency, in fact, it is the opposite. Intimacy is the ability to share your deepest, most private feelings, to have the strength to be vulnerable, to face the truth and to trust another without sacrificing your self or your identity. Such qualities require self-possession and self-esteem.

Dr. Wayne Dyer (2001) believes that to be intimate is to be tolerant and to accept another unconditionally. It means showing kindness and attuning yourself to the wants and needs of the other person. Such needs deserve the same respect as your own.

II. The Nature and Process of Relationships

A. A necessary condition for relationships

Self-love is a necessary condition for a healthy relationship. With self-love comes acceptance of the beloved with no demands, conditions or power plays. If we can answer the key questions of life namely are we loveable and are we loved, in the affirmative, all of our relations with others will be more positive and fulfilling.

M.J. Ryan (2004) writes: "If we expect someone or something outside ourselves to make us happy we lose our power. The truth is that we can't count on anything except our ability to choose how to respond to what happens to us." Therefore, to first look for love outside ourselves is to look for love in all the wrong places. You must first be introspective and conclude you are loveable because you are. Once you truly believe this, the love that has always surrounded you will become apparent. Only after this revelation and understanding will you be able to successfully share love with another on any level.

B. Our need to find fault in the other

"The Lion was a very good comrade for one so cowardly."
(The Wizard of Oz, 1900).

Groucho Marx famously stated that he would never join a club that would have him as a member. This attitude is similar to the one many share that "if he/she likes/loves me what's wrong with them?" Consciously or more often unconsciously this idea destroys many potential alliances and the cause is simply that we cannot fathom anyone loving us because we can't love ourselves.

Deepak Chopra (1997) writes: "We all step into the path of love out of need, but need can be self-destructive because its origins are feelings of inadequacy and fear of being alone." Any love or attraction based on feelings of insecurity which arise from the belief that we are unable to fulfill our own needs and that we must be taken care of to survive is immediately doomed. A person who seeks relationships only to gratify his or her own emotional or sexual needs, will find that each relationship is essentially identical and equally barren. To experience relationships of substance and depth requires approaching and entering them with a commitment and consideration for the other as well as a security in the self that allows sharing and acceptance.

C. Fear of intimacy and self-love

"I'm such a coward; but just as soon as they hear me roar, they all try to get away from me, and of course I let them go."
(Lion, The Wizard of Oz, 1900).

Realistically (oh, how we hate that word when it refers to relationships) we can't expect any one to love us more than we love ourselves. Furthermore, we can't expect anyone to fill the holes in our soul which we choose to create. We can only expect to have a fulfilling relationship, on any level, when we stop focusing on our needs and focus on those of the other.

The major stumbling block to loving completely is the fear of losing one's identity or one's very self. The fact is, the process of surrender and service to another strengthens self knowledge and therefore individual identity. Through this process your perspective changes from one of separation to one of unity. "In unity we perceive only love, express only love and are only love." (Chopra, 1997). Ultimately, we discover that we are worthy of love and respect simply because we exist as God's creation. We begin to celebrate the connection with another as we evolve into a "we" perspective. "The somebody waiting for you is always a reflection of yourself" continues Deepak Chopra (1997). Out of our loneliness, our needs, our feelings of lack, inadequacy and want, we seek a source of love that will fill the hole in the soul. "Whatever the need is, the person who fills it becomes the source of love."

D. <u>Beginning a relationship, leaving the past</u>

"Toto did not approve of the new comrade at first, for he could not forget how nearly he had been crushed between the Lion's great jaws; but after a time he became more at ease..."
(<u>The Wizard of Oz</u>, 1900).

Each relationship, casual to intimate, gives us occasion not only to learn more about ourselves but also to create a new self through caring, evolving and empathizing. Relationships are indeed our spiritual classroom but it is crucial to remember that with each new encounter we bring all of our past preconceptions, habits and biases. New people and new situations are neatly categorized based on old perspectives. We see and listen with distorted senses and judge with preconceived ideas. We tend not to take this moment to start anew but rather to confirm the old. Consequently, we neither grow nor achieve satisfaction. We smother an opportunity to discover in favor of confirming destructive biases and staying comfortably in the past. "The key to a right relationship..." writes Marianne Williamson (1992), "...and every situation is, in some way a relationship – is to allow each one, in every moment, to be lifted from the past. A relationship is reborn, whenever we see someone as they are right now and don't hold them to who they were. Focusing on the present and not the past is essential to experiencing love and understanding." Such focus is also crucial in fostering new partnerships.

Deepak Chopra (1997) likewise believes that the key for each connection is to focus on the now. He writes: "Up to the point when they merged, two lovers walked a separate path. Together they create a new path that has no past, where every step moves into the unknown..." It is precisely this unknown which so threatens us and destroys intimacy on all levels. Being exposed to a new perspective which encompasses new pleasures as well as new pains, panics us and we retreat to the comfort of the familiar. With patience, trust and acceptance this tragedy can be avoided and we can move forward, happier, more gratified and more enlightened.

E. Summary

A major conflict in our life journey is the simultaneous need for the other and the fear of attachment. Achieving a satisfactory association can involve a journey of pain, reflection, humility, acceptance and ultimately self-confirmation. To give and receive love, to be vulnerable yet protected and to learn as we teach are the rewards of a pleasurable, healthy and mature relationship.

Basic questions that should occur to people when they feel attracted to another while being simultaneously cautious and anxious are: Why did "fate" put this person in my life at this time? What can I learn? Can I become more fulfilled, content and wise with another than I can become alone? Will I be hurt, disappointed, used, and abused or will I realize more of my potential while nurturing and encouraging the potential of the other?

Relationships are probably the most frightening, challenging, frustrating yet rewarding part of our journey to wellness. Constructive partnerships on all levels are the ultimate consequences of learning, confidence and trust. Relationships provide opportunities to love and to grow, to live and to serve. As the Dalai Lama (1998) writes, "In addition to the beneficial effects on one's physical health, there is evidence that compassion and caring behaviors contribute to good emotional health." "An attitude of giving will attract more material and spiritual wealth than an attitude of getting" adds Marianne Williamson (2004). Observe those you consider spiritual and loving as they interact. Observe and learn. See and hear the mutual respect as their communication transpires.

A good rapport is a dance of mutual appreciation and respect. It requires gratitude, humility and acceptance. "Love is not love which alters when it alteration finds." (William Shakespeare). Relationships also require patience so that we may listen and courage so that we may release part of the "me" in order to participate in the "we". The goal is to understand, honor and nurture the other as we do ourselves. To love the self is a pre-requisite.

"People find themselves caught up in an anxious search for love precisely because they don't feel loveable" writes Deepak Chopra (1997). We must be comfortable in our own skin before we can begin to love. One can't give what one doesn't have. You must have love to give love. To relate in a genuine manner we must be able to laugh at ourselves and be vulnerable, so that we share and connect. Remember: "To forgive, to heal, to love is why we're here." (A Course in Miracles, 1976).

III. Impediments to Intimacy

"It is not our purpose to become each other; it is to recognize each other, to learn to see the other and respect them for what they are."
(Hermann Hesse, 1877 – 1962).

"If you cannot mould yourself entirely as you would wish how can you expect other people to be entirely to your liking?"
(Thomas A. Kempis, 1380 – 1471).

A. Expectations and disappointments

"Her friends were sorry but they could do nothing to help her..."
(The Wizard of Oz, 1900).

It is a rare person who when evaluating the potential for a more intimate relationship on any level doesn't include expectations. We are taught early on what is attractive and desirable. We are taught what we "deserve" and who would be "good for us." Like all past instruction and tutelage, the premises are based on the perspectives of others and how we play into their story. While the culture tells us what we need in someone and what is successful love, we hold our own expectations derived from the false beliefs of yesteryear.

Deepak Chopra (2004) writes about this phenomenon and how it contributes to much malaise as well as hampers growth and contentment. He writes that "...there is a restless kind of consumer shopping for partners, as if the 'right' one can be found by toting up…pluses and minuses until the number of pluses matches some mythical standard. The path to love, however, is never about externals. However good or bad you feel about your relationship, the person you are with at the moment is the 'right' person because he or she is a mirror of who you are inside."

Chopra (2004) goes on to explain that people commonly put satisfaction of their needs first when looking for a companion. Who can best fulfill us? Who can best make us whole? "When need dominates over love the fragile thread of spirit, 'us' is broken. When you 'fall' in love, you 'fall' for a mirror of your own present needs." For Chopra as for many spiritual teachers "need" implies "a lack in oneself, a missing piece that we mistakenly believe can be supplied by another. When this happens the lovers feel that the other can fill that space and are angry and disappointed when they cannot."

B. **Conditional love**

"I love you" is no longer an unconditional declaration writes Chopra. Our expectations of the other are high and we are easily disappointed. If we can't satisfy ourselves it is truly unrealistic to expect others to do so. Similarly, if we can't love ourselves neither can someone else, despite their best efforts. Therefore, when we look outside for self-fulfillment "I love you" becomes "I love you, if."

Dr. Chopra (1997) continues that when we "…focus on a needs based love/romance, the 'we' is distorted into becoming two 'me's' and the potential for growth is stifled. Each looks to fulfill their own needs and views the other as only another ally in this quest. What can you do for me as opposed to what can I do for you becomes the new mantra for love."

C. Fear of becoming vulnerable

"But she hugged the soft, stuffed body of the Scarecrow…and found she was crying herself at this sorrowful parting from her comrades."
(The Wizard of Oz, 1900).

To love is to be vulnerable. It is to surrender a certain amount of your emotional well being to the beloved because you care for them and share a part of their love. This creates a "we". If you cannot love yourself or be satisfied with yourself, your capacity to trust another and to become vulnerable is extremely limited. You are so afraid of being "found out" and you are so protective of your "self image" that you cannot see beyond yourself and relate.

To achieve intimacy you must be able to communicate your feelings and be willing to listen and to grow. How the other sees you is extremely important. To be a good and sensitive partner give up the need to be right for the right to be needed. Choose to be kind, to be understanding and to subjugate your desires. In short, you must serve the other. It is far better to be loving than to be correct.

D. Fear of losing the "I"

"'Send me back to Kansas, where my Aunt Em and Uncle Henry are,' she answered earnestly. 'I don't like your country, although it is so beautiful.'" (The Wizard of Oz, 1900).

The central issue confronting two beings wishing to form an intimate partnership is the consistent tension arising from the natural clash between the "I" that is "me" with the "I" that is "we". Both people forming a bond will throughout their time together be evaluating how much of themselves to give for the sake of the "we". If both partners have adequate self-esteem and believe in the other, these assessments are relatively painless. However, such circumstances are rare and generally occur only after two dedicated companions have developed the skills of

184

rapprochement, usually over a significant period of time. Each must be confident in themselves and secure in the other.

The most risky commitment is to a "we". Here we are most vulnerable. In the initial stages of attraction and attachment the couple is an "us". This is a rather amorphous association based on compatibility and a mutual magnetism. We like seeing the other, there are more wants than needs. As the relationship intensifies, desires increase, reliance on the other also increases and we begin to trust. The "I" is less protected and the "we" begins to form. The pleasure of being with the other exceeds the security of being alone.

How amenable we are to this metamorphosis depends on many factors, especially our upbringing. Primary caregivers were role models and the level of trust and regard they instilled resides in our psyche and determines to a certain degree our expectations and aspirations for our own alliances. How these early exemplars interacted, expressed emotion, tended to our needs etc., disposes us to expectations and comparisons.

Additionally, the capacity to incorporate any deviation from expectations and the ability to safeguard and nurture another, determine the ease of this transition. If one develops the necessary inner qualities such as humility, gratitude, acceptance and trust, the progression from the "I" to the "we" will be much smoother. As we live in love, wisdom and courage, the need to protect the "I" decreases dramatically and we begin to embrace the "we" and discard the "us". The "I" is redefined and we develop a more inclusive and secure world view.

E. Control vs. surrender

"For, of course, if Dorothy stops here she will never get back to Kansas." (The Wizard of Oz, 1900).

Of course for all of this to transpire, we must give up the delusion of control. This is the central appeal in the "Serenity" Prayer. Coping with change and knowing what we can do about it are life issues which are never fully resolved. However, as we pursue wisdom, we learn to negotiate transition and to become more comfortable with surrendering and trusting the outcome of events to a higher power.

You should begin to appreciate change as a path to growth, rather than a danger to the self and your world view. Be open to each moment as an opportunity to learn something new about yourself and your world. Focus on the needs of the other and what you can give to the relationship. It will be returned ten fold. To bond positively with another, we must subordinate the ego/child-self's needs and wants. Your only motive now becomes to love and to serve. As Deepak Chopra (2004) writes: "Surrender is the door one must pass through to find passion."

F. Vulnerability as a delusion

"When we have climbed over the wall we shall know what is on the other side." (Dorothy, The Wizard of Oz, 1900).

We now progress from understanding and delineating the behavioral changes necessary to bring the concepts of "I" and "we" closer, to uncovering the internal change of perspective needed to reduce the fear of vulnerability in all levels of connection. First, we must change our frame of reference regarding the "I" especially as it relates to any relationship. Our early years have imposed a definition of "I", which has become part of our self-concept. This characterization has distorted the expectations of future relationships in addition to the role we play in soliciting and sustaining them.

Key questions emerge as to who we are and what is our capacity to relate to others. What projections come to mind? Why are we anxious? Why do we want to be more intimate? The best strategy in the face of the apprehension raised by these questions, is to suspend attempts to answer and to slowly move forward with the perspective and approach of a participant/observer. As we progress, we redefine ourselves and our expectations of the other and of the "we". We are presented with choices leading to changes which lead to more choices. With love, gratitude, acceptance and humility, we can build an alliance which will assure mutual growth and contentment. As trust proliferates, we discover that vulnerability is a delusion which only served the purpose of maintaining the status quo. Ironically as we allow ourself to bond we simultaneously allow ourselves to be free.

You can neither find nor give love unless you allow yourself to receive love. Immutable boundaries and the child-self must be discarded. Openness and trust need to permeate the "me". Surrender your defenses and have the inner strength and self-esteem to allow yourself to be vulnerable to love. The desire for the status quo and the fear of change will loudly tell you that you are not worthy of love or that there must be something wrong with anyone who would love you. In order to receive love you must give love in every area of your life. You must be willing to risk, to take a small step forward for progress and contentment. Trust!

G. Projection, defensiveness and vulnerability

"'I understand how you feel,' said the little girl, who was truly sorry for him.'" (The Wizard of Oz, 1900).

Often when you are offended, it is because you have constructed arbitrary rules as to how you should be treated (very possibly you were taught such rules by those early arbiters of your identity) and, therefore you are reluctant to challenge such rules. When you are offended, rather than identifying the broken rule and attempting to understand, you choose to separate and isolate yourself behind a barrier of righteous indignation, preventing any opportunity for tolerance. From such a stance one mistakenly attempts to gain a sense of superiority by minimizing vulnerability and inclusion while maximizing isolation, exclusion and control.

Such defensiveness manifests itself when we argue passionately, raise our voices, become physical etc. In short, we are being self-protective when we become enraged and lose control so as to conceal our fear. Recognizing this can be an opportunity to cool down, to take a moment and begin to learn about ourselves. Instead, we impulsively plunge forward always attempting to justify the unjustifiable. We no longer hear the other because we are too threatened to listen. The focus and intent become absolving anger rather than acknowledging the cries of our companion.

This is the greatest threat to communication and consequently one of the more significant obstacles to achieving a fulfilling, mutually healthy relationship on any level. If we practice humility, defensiveness and anger become a learning opportunity regarding who we are versus who we are pretending to be. When we become defensive, it is in response to a perceived threat. The "I" versus the "them" must be replaced by a redefinition of the partnership and of the "we" and "us". All toxic tendencies are created by internal conflicts rummaging for release in randomly chosen external events. Incoherent thought and emotional tension become expressed by way of impulsive and destructive deeds. Blame and accusation are then employed to put a veneer of rationality on the absurd.

Therefore be aware of your disposition to be defensive when in discussions. Be humble. Be willing to hear the other's viewpoint as a legitimate critique about your behavior. See the difference of opinion objectively, as an opportunity to learn. Disagreements are healthy attempts to refine the "we" so as to include each "I". Effective communication is a process which involves much work and sacrifice but it is a vital component for progression toward fulfillment.

H. Summary

Expectations of ourselves, the other and the relationship ("we") are frequently excessive, illogical and illusory. The degree to which we are not functioning individually with wisdom, love and courage is the degree to which we will be dissatisfied with ourselves and our partners. Trouble is inevitable when we strive to fill the needs of the self by means of a relationship which pursues someone else for solutions.

Another obstacle to intimacy is our fear of being hurt if we allow ourselves to care and trust another on any level. This fear of vulnerability is also a reflection of low self-esteem and a desire to maintain the status quo through isolation and denial. As we begin to live while nurturing and practicing the seven spiritual qualities of humility, gratitude, acceptance/forgiveness, patience/trust, wisdom, love and courage, such resistance will pass and a desire to form a relationship will surface.

Fear of being hurt, is compounded by fear of losing the self, as the "I" merges partially into the "we". This apprehension is based on the unrealistic assumption that a partnership represents an "either", "or" situation and that changing part of the "I" to form a "we" will be destructive. That misconception must be overcome so that we may evolve and learn.

We desperately hold on to the past when confronted with change. Change by definition is an alteration or modification which often results in stress. If we see the universe as benign and that each situation has a purpose, we can begin to trust, accept and surrender. If we are to achieve contentment, this is the ideal approach to life.

Relationships represent a unique opportunity to embrace spirit and to expand knowledge, experience and potential for development. Like all new adventures there are both risks and rewards. As we reconstruct our consciousness, a perspective of service and love, acceptance and trust will maximize the rewards while courage and wisdom will minimize the risks.

IV. Relationship Skills

The ultimate challenge with relationships at all levels is when to stay and when to go. If you have infused your friendships with love, acceptance and patience then you have done all that you can. Not to do these things and utilize these temperaments is to prevent either partner from fully developing. To make a decision about the cessation of a relationship without considering all alternatives is to smother growth and to judge without all of the evidence.

The following presents several behavioral and attitudinal approaches to nurturing, maintaining, protecting and perpetuating all types of associations against the natural child-self tendencies to preserve the status quo through fear, aggression and control.

A. <u>Caring behaviors</u>

> *"Do let me carry that basket for you. I shall not mind it, f or I can't get tired." (Scarecrow, <u>The Wizard of Oz</u>, 1900).*

> *"Appreciation is a wonderful thing: it makes what is excellent in others belong to us as well." (Voltaire, 1768).*

Behaviors that make the other feel valued, understood, safe, and accepted, practiced on a regular basis, are the best guarantors of preserving the relationship, building intimacy and avoiding confrontation and strife. This is not easy. It requires sensitivity to them in all interactions and discussions. Furthermore, we have to enhance our humility, and expand our gratitude, acceptance and patience. We must listen to understand rather than to judge or censure. We should cherish and nurture, compliment and be kind. We need to touch to be gentle and to reassure. We should look to give, not get, to serve and not to be served. At each opportunity, choose the positive, the loving and the enriching. If we are aware of how precious they are and the important role partners have in our lives and if we are intent on showing this, we will succeed.

B. <u>Communication skills</u>

Be aware of how you express feelings both verbally and behaviorally. Each phrase and gesture communicates something unique. Pay attention and don't be defensive, so that you may learn and appreciate what the other person is saying. Be precise and thoughtful in responses and expressions. Infuse all communication with unconditional positive regard. Remember "namaste"; "I cherish the place where you and I are one."

You will immediately identify ineffective communication when you begin to feel anger and find yourself using sentences beginning with "You". Now you are becoming an accuser instead of a facilitator. You may even wag your finger and raise your voice. Such signs should immediately signal that your efforts are not achieving their objective.

Especially in stressful times all expressions and elucidations should begin with "I". In order to clarify a point you can legitimately only speak for yourself. Ideally, when undertaking this task, you will not only formulate and illuminate your thoughts and feelings for yourself but also for your partner. Self-statements are open to a minimum of legitimate rebuttal because you are genuinely enunciating your personal perceptions. Remember most of all:

1. You can make your point without being angry.

2. Listen to understand.

3. It is better to love than to conquer.

4. If anger dominates, have the courage and foresight to take a time out.

5. Always speak from the "I" perspective.

6. Avoid "shoulds," "woulds" and "coulds".

7. Stay in the present moment; do not invoke past history or pain.

8. Stay on the issue; do not generalize or get off point.

9. Never invoke family members to make your point.

10. Do not let impulse rule logic.

C. <u>Compromise</u>

"'This is all true,' said Dorothy, 'and I am glad I was of use to these good friends.'" (<u>The Wizard of Oz</u>, 1900).

Don't be afraid to be wrong, misunderstood or misled. Don't fear the other's hurt or anger by being defensive. Seek commonalities not differences. Attempt to join not to separate. Aspire and endeavor to underscore and define the "we" not the "I". This is not being subservient but rather nurturing the "we" so that the "I" may grow.

During disagreements, if we are to succeed in refining relationships the goal should be to understand the other's perspective rather than having them understand ours. If we realize that both points are valid, this awareness will be less a chore and more a lesson in patience, acceptance, trust and humility. Allow personal space, allow time and allow love. Such a process will ultimately reveal a middle where both parties can feel acceptance and respect.

D. <u>Damage control</u>

"Everything that irritates us about others, can lead us to an understanding of ourselves." (Carl Jung, 1925).

When all else fails and impulse overrules logic, when the "I" supersedes the "we" and when isolation is chosen over acceptance, damage control is the strategy of choice. Many psychologists believe that we argue in order to distance ourselves from each other, to strengthen the "I" and redefine the "we" so as to set up semi-permanent boundaries until the disputed issues are resolved.

"A disagreement is like a cut on the skin" writes Marianne Williamson (2002). "You need to treat it gently and not cut further. So it should be, when we see things differently, that gentleness guides our speech." If we begin to experience anger it means that we are being defensive. We attempt to defend self-image, self-esteem, our version of reality and/or world view. Once defensiveness takes over due to fear, we discard love, caring, communication, compromise and acceptance as the child-self rules. The disagreement becomes an argument, an "I" versus "thee"; a dual to the death. "Emotional havoc usually comes not from the issues that divide us so much as from the things we say and do due to the issues that divide us." (Williamson, 2002).

The bottom line is that the degree to which we feel threatened and afraid is the degree to which we will become defensive and angry. Williamson (2002) continues on this exact point "... it's not our disagreements that wound but rather the criticism, attack and blame..." So force yourself to step back, take a breath and try to regain the feeling of love and understanding, instead of anger, fear and insecurity.

It is crucial to remember that when we respond to dispute with anger, the child-self conquers. If possible picture a huge baby with a pacifier and rattle, extremely red in the face and having a tantrum. That is you. Arguments and disagreements when viewed from a loving perspective are opportunities to relate and learn. One can embrace and accept the other as well as accept and embrace the self. The "we" has greater potential for self-growth and contentment than the "I".

The "other" was put into our life for a reason. This partner is our teacher and we are mutually obligated to reach out, surrender our defenses and tune in. The most important person to your wellness may be an arm's length away.

E. Identifying projection and anger

"Projection" is a term used by therapists to define a tendency that people have such that traits, emotions, characteristics etc. which they dislike in themselves and do not want to admit to having are "projected" (attributed to) another. Consequently, what we find most annoying about someone else may be the precise trait that we have but are unwilling to acknowledge. Projection can be a rationalization to avoid responsibility for progress and to justify isolation and self-pity.

Deepak Chopra (2004) writes: "Projection always hides a feeling that you don't want to look at. If you examine any negative trait that you insist exists in another person you will find the same trait hiding in yourself. The more you deny this trait the more strongly you will have to project it." He goes on to write, "What you hate most in others, you most strongly deny in yourself. This is a spiritual lesson that we try to evade by projecting, blaming, and making excuses for ourselves." The person we hate most is our best teacher.

So resist the temptation to look outward, instead be brave and look inward when there are disputes. Be responsible for your behavior and emotions. Don't be an accountant looking for inconsistencies, pointing out each flaw, every annoyance. The fault lies in you. Marianne Williamson (2002) sums this up best. "While we are born with a perfect capacity to love, each of us is tempted by the realities of life to withhold our love and defend against pain." Once we are hurt and we become aware of our vulnerability, listening and understanding become secondary to our need for safety. Therefore, cease the destructive dance of defensiveness, listen in order to love and learn, resist fear and have the courage to be vulnerable. This is extremely difficult but absolutely necessary if we are to achieve our life's goal of growth and contentment.

V. Summary

Relationship Skills

A crucial question as we pursue maturation and serenity is, how rewarding and stable are our relationships? Generally, the less personal the association the easier it is to be consistent and compatible. As relationships become more intimate the issue frequently becomes, is it worth the time and emotional energy to pursue or should we move on? This is a difficult question because so much toxic sentiment interferes with logical consideration. Therefore, it is helpful in the quest for personal integration, to master some basic skills. These will provide essential information necessary to our decision making process. This chapter elucidates such skills in the hope that the reader will not only optimize current affiliations but also will be better able to become a participant-observer in this crucial facet of their lives.

VI. For Further Consideration

1. Relationships are defined to include the most casual nod of recognition to the intense, intimate dance one has with a lover.

2. Ideally relationships can become the key to contentment and self-knowledge.

3. A successful and rewarding relationship is a primary objective of self-fulfillment.

4. Crucial qualities one should practice for any successful relationship are patience/ trust, acceptance, humility, forgiveness and gratitude.

5. Intimate and rewarding interpersonal relationships are necessary for mental health.

6. To be intimate on any level is to have the courage to be vulnerable.

7. We must learn to accept and love ourselves before we can give acceptance and love to another.

8. One must put the needs of another ahead of one's own for a successful relationship. How may I give versus what can I get?

9. The "other" can be our greatest teacher especially about ourselves.

10. When we enter into a new association on any level we always bring our past baggage. Ultimately, this must be left behind or at least checked if we are to move forward.

11. Relationships can be improved by the willingness and intent to use skills such as caring behaviors, communication skills, compromise and damage control.

12. To succeed in all levels of intimacy we must address two questions: Are we loveable and are we loved?

13. A major conflict is the simultaneous need to be close and protected while independent and self-sustaining.

14. Constructive relations on any level are a by-product of living a life of love, wisdom, and courage.

15. As we attempt to define a new, more intimate relationship, another conflict for both parties becomes the clash between the "I" that is "me" with the "I" that is "we".

16. Understanding and accepting the role of control in our life is essential to all healthy friendships as well as to a contented life.

17. Being personally offended is usually caused by arbitrary rules which we were taught and we now use to judge our partnerships and interactions.

18. Being defensive which involves inward fear and outward anger is a primary barrier to intimacy and communication.

19. Disagreements, discussions and arguments can be healthy attempts to redefine the "we" so as to include a less threatened "I".

20. Be aware that it is not unusual to unconsciously "project" distasteful traits. Therefore, what we dislike in ourselves but deny, we tend to see in another.

Part IV

Love, Wisdom and Courage:

A Spiritual Nexus

". . . the greatest loss I had known was the loss of my heart." (Tin Man).

"It is such an uncomfortable feeling to know one is a fool."
(Scarecrow).

"All the other animals in the forest expect me to be brave, for the
Lion is everywhere thought to be the King of the Beasts."

(The Wizard of Oz, 1900).

The Ultimate Goal

Spiritual leaders and influential philosophers of both Eastern and Western traditions have stressed the necessity of a life ruled by love, courage and wisdom. This is the ultimate achievement of self-actualization and results from the continual practice of humility, gratitude, patience and acceptance in every aspect of our lives. While love is the emotional expression of wisdom and wisdom the intellectual expression of love, courage is the attribute that triggers action, energizes behavior and propels us to interact with the outside world.

Each of Dorothy's companions represent one of these virtues. Ironically, it is demonstrated throughout the novel that each possessed and utilized the very virtue that they sought from the Wizard. When Oz pretended to bestow these virtues, the Tin Man, the Lion and the Scarecrow did what they always had done but now with increased intent and awareness. With the external validation provided by Oz, they had the confidence to be themselves, as they were created to be.

At the end of the novel, prior to returning to Kansas, Dorothy displays each of the attributes. She wisely chooses to go home after listening to the good witch Glinda. She expresses love and concern for her comrades as well as Aunt "Em" and Uncle Henry. She shows courage by her willingness to accept empowerment and begin another journey into the unknown as she returns to Kansas. Dorothy has now completed this part of her journey in Oz and is starting again in Kansas with all the wisdom, love and courage derived from her experiences.

Chapter 10

On Loving and Being Loved

"All you need is love." (John Lennon).

*"The supreme happiness of life is the conviction that we are loved;
loved for ourselves, or rather in spite of ourselves."
(Victor Hugo, 1862).*

I. Definition

The Oxford Pocket Dictionary and Thesaurus (American Edition, 1997) defines "love" as "n. (1) a deep affection; fondness; (2) sexual passion." As a transitive verb it is defined as "(1) feel love or deep fondness for; (2) delight in, admire, greatly cherish." The Random House Webster's Dictionary (Fourth Edition 2001) defines "love" – "n.(1) a profoundly tender, passionate affection for another person; (2) an intense personal attachment; (3) a strong enthusiasm or liking."

Acceptable synonyms include devotion, attraction, friendship, adoration as well as liking, enjoyment, preference, concern, care.

This chapter will refer to "love" in a less carnal, passionate usage and more in the "attraction" and "devotion" sense.

A. <u>Love and power</u>

"'No, my head is quite empty,' answered the Woodman; 'but once I had brains, and a heart also; so, having tried them both, I should much rather have a heart.'" (<u>The Wizard of Oz</u>, 1900).

"An authentically empowered person lives in love. Love is the energy of the soul. Love is what heals the personality." writes Gary Zukov in <u>Seat of the Soul</u> (1999). He goes on to opine: "Love is not a passive state. It is an active force. It is the force of the soul. Love does more than bring peace where there is conflict. It brings a different way of being in the world. It brings harmony and an active interest in the well being of others."

Historically three types of love have been distinguished: 1) sexual love which frequently involves possession and control ("Eros") 2) friendship, attraction and general affection with no sexual intimacy ("Philos") and 3) an unconditional love and compassion for all ("Agape"). In truth there is only a love composed of humility, gratitude and acceptance. Variations of love are experienced depending upon the presence and level of Eros. As used in the context of this work, "love" is defined simultaneously as gratitude, humility and acceptance each separate yet each working together to produce a synergism which alters feeling, behavior, thought, and life perspective. Above all, such a metamorphosis also requires awareness, intention and self-discipline.

II. The Daily Struggle to Find and Express Love

"While I was in love I was the happiest man on earth; but no one can love who has not a heart, so I am resolved to ask Oz to give me one." (Tin Man, The Wizard of Oz, 1900).

A. Love vs. fear

Marianne Williamson writes in A Return to Love (1992): "Love is what we were born with. Fear is what we learned here." Our spiritual journey is the relinquishment and unlearning of fear while accepting love back into our hearts. To express love we have to return to trust and risk rejection. There is no way in which we can feel complete and content that does not include expressing love in all its forms.

Unfortunately we would rather be safe than loving. It is easier to remain wrapped in a blanket of defensiveness than to reach out and show caring and respect for another. It is indeed possible if we make such an outreach that the others will respond with fear and ignore, reject, or mock us. The stronger their reaction against love the greater their fear. They are rejecting love and not us. But even knowing this we still resist. We prefer standing on the sideline watching, perhaps wishing the first move will be theirs and falsely believing that we can control acceptance and rejection. No risk, no fear; no action, no growth.

When we do attain love, fear no longer dominates. A new paradigm prevails. We would rather be rejected than not reach out. We become brave and trusting in ourselves. Acceptance dominates and we see ourselves and others as deserving respect and love. We begin to understand that extending love is not dependent on whether the other is "worthy" or loveable; rather it depends upon our level of acceptance, trust and compassion. We must reach this point for the sake of all. "Love and compassion are necessities not luxuries. Without them, humanity cannot survive." (Dalai Lama, 1998).

B. Fear and the "child-self"

"Love cannot attack." (A Course in Miracles, 1976).

"If you truly loved yourself, you would never hurt another."
(Buddha, 523 BCE).

If we are born with loving hearts and fear of expressing that love is learned, from whom is it learned? Our identity and worldview are handed down from previous generations who were sometimes suspicious of "outsiders" and were afraid of expressing or even acknowledging many of their own emotions. Their influence was exacted on us before comprehension, questioning, understanding, or experience could take place.

As infants we were unformed clay begging to be shaped by any "authority" figure who would take the time to impose their beliefs and embrace us. When, how, and where our issues originated we cannot remember. We only believe. To doubt, even when events give us the evidence, rouses fear and discomfort. So we blindly continue in our apprehension and ignorance as we resist the opportunities that each day brings, to question, learn and grow. We disregard the chance to become empowered by facing truth and behaving in ways which benefit all. As the status quo prevails, isolation and the child-self predominate.

C. Opportunities

"Love grows by giving. The love we give away is the only love we keep. The only way to retain love is to give it away."
(Elbert Hubbard, 1856-1915).

Every day with each interaction we can choose to advance love or reinforce fear. According to many spiritual teachers love consists of, but is not limited to, the four essential traits of spirituality namely humility, gratitude, acceptance/forgiveness, and patience/trust. Every expression of these is a reflection of love. Each in turn, generates kindness, compassion, tenderness and mercy. We decide which we will express and when. Our power lives in choosing love over fear, acceptance over isolation, the "we" over the "I". Awareness and intent practiced daily will spur us to choose correctly. We will lead a contented life when we are predisposed to act on our loving inclinations instead of the aggression and narcissism based on avoidance and ignorance. Love is learning, it is the greatest learning of the soul.

D. <u>Love and awareness</u>

"Your task is not to seek love, but merely to seek and find all the barriers within yourself that you have built against love."
(Jalal Ud-Din Rumi 1207-1273 A.D.).

We must expand our vision to behold the blessings before us. We are like children, cowering and covering our eyes when we are afraid. We refuse to see what is, because it presents challenges. The challenge we fear is the challenge of change. We cling, we defer, we die. The tragedy of our lives is not the mistakes we made but that we never tried. We refused to trust, to see and to grow. Again and again we are offered love. The time is now to accept.

Awareness and intent are the guides. As you read this, you can decide to loosen the chains of the child-self and live a life of contentment and peace. Now is the time that you can intend love and freedom or remain in your self-protective shell living a life of isolation, greed, and fictitious control. Be informed that:

1. You can choose.

2. The only choice is between love and fear.

3. You can control the choice but not the result.

4. This opportunity is always present with each interaction.

5. When you intend love the decision about

which choice to make will become clear.

6. You must continually work to improve both awareness and intent.

7. With each event or interaction stop, take three deep breaths assess the situation and choose the path to follow.

Just as we are taught what makes us laugh and what offends, what is beautiful and what is beastly, we can learn how to serve and how to love. It is time to relearn and rediscover our loving, accepting, and trusting nature. Ask for God's help to see beauty, to see yourself in another, to be loving and kind rather than right and righteous.

E. <u>Love and power</u>

". . . love is the power to choose between the wise and unwise."
(Sri Krishna, <u>Buddha Is As Buddha Does</u>, 2007).

Once again we see the power of the reciprocal relationship. Humility, gratitude, patience, and acceptance generate love which in turn reinforces the expression of these essential tools of spirituality. As Dr. Lorne Lander write in <u>The Lost of Art of Compassion</u> (2004): "Love, then is not to be viewed as something soft or weak. Love has power, some may argue that it is the most powerful force in the universe. We survive through connection and are destroyed by division. Love provides that glue; it is the matrix of being."

Unfortunately the countervailing force, the child-self, is also extremely powerful and fights for domination. This is the struggle that is the human condition. The power of love versus the power of the child-self and fear. Once we understand that the capacity to choose will always be ours and that there are only two very clear choices (love or fear) we can begin to restructure our life for expansion and peace. As Teilhard de Chardin (1881-1955) writes: "Love is the affinity which links and draws together the elements of the world . . ."

III. Limitless Love

*"Of all the gods, Love is the best friend of humankind, the helper
and the healer of all ills that stand in the way
of human happiness." (Plato, 427-347 B.C.).*

*"Toto played all day long, and Dorothy played with him,
and loved him dearly." (The Wizard of Oz, 1900).*

Although the practice of awareness and intent is extremely
important as we transact our daily routines, a more permanent
perspective encompassing love-mindedness is necessary to
consistently achieve contentment. We must assimilate an attitude
of love as part of our very being, in order to succeed. The power
of love has no limits and we need to participate in that power.

A. The ultimate question

*"Love is not idealization, it is acceptance. Humility is at
the heart leading to love." (Deepak Chopra, 1997).*

As we deliberate the question of our appeal and desirability,
ultimately we should reach a point of humble and grateful
self-acceptance. This is not complacency or conceit nor does
it end the quest to initiate and respond to love. Rather it is
a quiet, tranquil sensation that embraces "being" rather than
chasing "becoming." It is the result of practicing an awareness
of love which eventually culminates into a more encompassing
perspective. This is a function of time, motivation, and intent.
It will evolve in its own way while we progress and begin to
genuinely love ourselves, developing, nurturing and refining the
four necessary components of love.

This feeling of self-acceptance is one of soul serenity, and
quiet confidence. You believe at that moment you are where you
should be as a participant in the greater scheme of things. You are
part of a divine whole. You are confident that your feelings and
actions will produce connectedness and peace. These feelings and

behaviors are promoting similar reactions in those you encounter. This is the result of your awareness and intention. You are now experiencing the synergy of love, courage, and wisdom. It is a major shift in perception that results from the consistent practice of humility, gratitude, acceptance and patience. This sensation appears to be analogous to "rapture" and described by some religious congregations as occurring during their services. It is the miracle that awaits us. We know we are lovable and we see the love that embraces us.

B. <u>Love and emotional development</u>

"Try to treat with equal love all people whom you have relations. Thus the abyss between 'myself' and 'yourself' will be filled in; this is the goal of all religious worship."
(Sri Anandamayi Ma, 1896-1982).

As we develop, we understand that the two critical life questions: ("Are we loveable?" and "Are we loved?") can be reduced to "Are we loveable?" Once this is convincingly answered humbly and gratefully in the affirmative we see love everywhere. Our eyes open to more than desires and wants. The child-self is vanquished to its room and told to sleep. Our new journey in discovery begins and all our awareness is revitalized and renewed. "When you find love you find yourself." (Deepak Chopra, 2004).

Now we realize and master the truism that we keep something by giving it away. We serve ourselves by serving others. What positive emotions we offer the universe are returned many fold. We understand and we live by the belief that every encounter is sacred and an opportunity to learn. We know that in others we see ourselves both good and bad. We learn, then we embrace. Again the power of reciprocity is realized. As our love, respect, and compassion for humanity intensifies so it does for ourselves which in turn generates more love and caring. This is the cycle of love to which we aspire. "What makes you happy is not the love that other people feel for you, but the love you feel for other people." (Don Miguel Ruiz, The Voice of Knowledge, 2004). This is the shift in perspective; this is the miracle of growth and contentment.

C. Love and letting go of control

"Love seeketh not itself to please,
Nor for itself hath any care;
But for another gives its ease
And builds a Heaven in Hell's despair."
(William Blake, 1757-1827).

As we internalize the axiom that to give is to receive, we begin to recognize that it is not in our power to control another no matter how intense or intimate the interconnection may be. In fact, the more personal the relationship and the more needy we are, the more control becomes a restriction to love and caring. Control erodes and eventually destroys, trust, patience and acceptance. It causes the other to slip away. Attempts at control only increase the instability between two people. It is like greasing a hand so you may hold it more tightly.

Due to self-hate and insecurities, we are afraid to let people grow and evolve. The truth is that we must accept the beloved "as is" and let go of the need to confine, change and control or the relationship will be decimated. Love is not about managing another, it is about acceptance and appreciation. To love is to see someone as a person to be cherished because they are our great teacher and they choose to love us.

When we live love we do not judge or compare, rather we focus on what we like, what makes us smile and feel warm and fuzzy. The other person is God's gift for our own individual growth. We must listen, understand, and accept what is said so that we can develop positively. Ultimate transformation can only come from change that is generated by the relationship evolving and maturing. Love is personified by the person in front of us because they freely choose to be there. Our goal when we are living love is to cherish what we see and to be grateful for the presence and insight of our beloved. "Love isn't love until it's 'unconditional'" (Marianne Williamson, A Return to Love, 1992). When we experience and nurture this kind of love, on any physical level, we reach as close as possible to heaven on earth.

D. Love as life's unifying dynamic

"I am a Woodman, and made of tin. Therefore, I have no heart and cannot love. I pray you give me a heart that I may be as other men are." (Woodman, The Wizard of Oz, 1900).

Our goal is to reach a style and manner of living so that all our thoughts, feelings and behaviors are motivated by a combination of love, courage, and wisdom as we adapt and adjust to each encounter. Love on this level, is the emotional embodiment of wisdom, expressed and energized by courage. It has the synergistic power of unifying the most potent forces in the universe.

Teilhard de Chardin (1881-1955) writes of this interconnection between love and energy. He believes that the spirit generated by love can unite all people because "it alone joins all of us by what is deepest in ourselves." As we achieve self-acceptance, we develop a more subtle and powerful form of love that transcends physical boundaries and desire. We begin to accept our union and community with everyone as we simultaneously experience uniqueness and worth. We are humbled to be in such formidable company yet proud that we contribute and make a positive difference as part of the whole. Now we are on a spiritual plane of thought, feeling, and behavior. We know and sense the sanctity of the Universe. Love has transformed us and carried us to a higher level of being, "...a truly evolved being is one that values others more than it values itself, and that values love more than

212

the physical world and what's in it." Gary Zukov, (<u>The Seat of the Soul</u>, 1999).

IV. Impediments to Love

"I think you are wrong to want a heart. It makes most people unhappy. If you only knew it, you are in luck not to have a heart." *(Oz to Tin Man, <u>The Wizard of Oz</u>, 1900).*

"For my part I will bear all the unhappiness without a murmur, if you will give me the heart." (Tin Man <u>The Wizard of Oz</u>, 1900).

The closer we come to our goal of genuine spiritual love which is the pinnacle of emotional development, the stronger and more powerful the child-self becomes, kicking and screaming as it resists its own demise.

A. Fear

"To fear love is to fear life, and those who fear life are already three parts dead." (Bertrand Russell, 1872-1970).

Our sole, spiritual mission in life is to extend and expand love in ourselves and in others. It is to serve and mitigate suffering. Fear is at the core of dysfunction and the most severe restraint to advancement. Our ultimate purpose on this earth is to promote mutually loving, compassionate relationships as well as to enhance respect, caring, and empathy for ourselves and others. We must loosen the shackle of the "I" so that "we" and "us" become the most consequential aspect of our identity. Ultimately, "them" is incorporated by "us" to then become "we," as isolation, rejection, and hatred dissipate. Do not deny yourself the experience of love. Rather, cherish its multiple flavors and colors. Embrace the fragrance and the caress of this intimate melody; this dance of discovery and tenderness.

Fear comes in many forms and guises. It is constantly

morphed by our own rationalizations and self-deceptions. Most notably it serves stagnation. It hampers movement and growth. Fear can feel distinctly different in each instance but its effect is the same. It spawns isolation, arrogance, aggression, envy, and apathy. Each is unique but each is based on fear. As Marianne Williamson (2002) writes: "Fear is our shared lovelessness, our individual and collective hells. When fear is expressed, we recognize it as anger, abuse, disease, pain, greed, addiction, selfishness, obsession, corruption, violence, and war."

We must reduce this power of the child-self and allow love and trust to enter our hearts. Courage is the solution. Surrender and acceptance are the means. "Denying love is the only problem, and embracing it is the only answer." (A Course in Miracles, 1976).

B. Culture

"Love looks through a telescope, envy through a microscope."
(Josh Billups, 1818-1885).

Envy, arrogance and pride are each culturally inculcated. We learn status, stratum, and grouping through the persistent assault of advertising and the advice and counsel of peers and mentors. We become what we have and we demean others if they don't have the same things. We will never be satisfied because we focus on the external. We perceive only yearning and feel only frustration as we seek the latest cure or prize. We create our own jails as we curse the imprisonment spurred by consumerism. Happiness is close at hand; just jump a little higher, crawl a little longer. "Meaning doesn't lie in things. Meaning lies in us. When we attach value to things that aren't love, the money, the car, the house, the prestige, we are loving things that can't love us back. We are searching for meaning in the meaningless." (Williamson, 1992).

Love, wisdom, and courage can free us. This spiritual, intellectual, and emotional triumvirate can emancipate us from the incessant domination of the child-self. They can lead us

214

out of self-imposed physical and psychological limits to a state of objective observation. We can have the courage to embrace truth, the love to conquer fear and the wisdom to see beyond ourselves. This takes time and diligence but it is possible.

C. <u>Our history</u>

"'All the same,' said the Scarecrow, 'I shall ask for brains instead of heart; for a fool would not know what to do with a heart if he had one.'"

"'I shall take the heart' returned the Tin Woodsman, 'for brains do not make one happy, and happiness is the best thing in the world.'"
(<u>The Wizard of Oz</u>, 1900).

We are taught to think in terms of such dichotomies. Is it black or white, good or evil, friend or foe? In the spiritual realm of unity, there are no such separations or disagreements. All is one. We are part of a supreme whole which is perfect. Each piece seamlessly merges with the other in unison. We are also informed about whether and how we are loved and loveable. We are taught the qualities and characteristics of those we should love and those who should love us. Unfortunately, we are also apprised as to how we are deficient, and how we have disappointed and failed to meet others' expectations.

In our world of the physical, there is success and failure, love and hate. Some say that we must be careful in giving love and suspicious about the receiving it. Love is something to be earned, to be worthy of. Such caution serves only to confine and confuse. As love reaches out we recoil. We question why, who would love us. Love from others is awkward when we have yet to learn to love ourselves. Once again this is fear in disguise. Self-hate protects us from anguish because we isolate, languish, and fester, rather than reach out and risk. "We can find a lot of different ways to express how much we hate ourselves. Turned inward, it becomes our personal hells: addiction, obsession, compulsion, depression, violent relationships, illness." (Williamson, 1992).

Self-hate, self-destruction, low self-esteem, depression, whatever the label, is just another mindset to separate us from our spiritual essence. How can you cultivate love in a field of self-hate? You can't give what you don't have and you can't have what you don't feel. If you are taught you are deficient, deprived and disabled, you cannot perceive the abundance, benevolence, or competence that encompasses you.

God makes no mistakes. Each day in every way we can choose to get better and stronger. We can choose to pursue our goal of spiritual mindedness. Each day we must review our Personal Development Program and start anew. We must strive to fulfill our destiny, to be all we can and overpower self-imposed barriers. We must work to self-affirm and begin the minute steps necessary to reach our goals. Offer and accept a compliment without qualification or question, reach out, be yourself, embrace life and you will shed your past destructive delusions.

V. Summary

"What does love look like? It has hands to help others. It has feet to hasten to the poor and needy. It has eyes to see misery and want. It has ears to hear the sighs and sorrows of humankind. That is what love looks like." (St. Augustine of Hippo, 410 A.D.).

Love is the third goal of ideal spiritual living which includes wisdom and courage. Love is the emotional reflection and articulation of wisdom. Love and wisdom, although independent entities, converge, coalesce, and combine to generate an all encompassing "love mindedness." Such a perspective gives us the strength and insight to react and interact in a manner that generates joy, compassion, and benevolence.

Our destiny in life is self-fulfillment; to become what we were created to be. As a flower must blossom, so we must become. This is realized as we are released from fear to live a life of love. Forgiveness, acceptance, kindness, compassion, validation, empowerment, and approval are choices we make, each moment, with each interaction, every day. We have to increase our awareness of such opportunities, and with intent and self-discipline respond in a compassionate way. We must make this happen. The Golden Rule is to love one another and to treat others as we wish to be treated. We must no longer simply wish but we must act. The change we want to see should first become the change within us. We need to be what we want to see in others.

VI. For Further Consideration

". . . the greatest loss I had known was the loss of my heart."
(Tin Woodsman, The Wizard of Oz, 1900).

1. Love is defined in many ways from "fondness" to "consummate oneness." The definition depends on the level of physical desire and self/other boundaries. Love is always composed of humility, gratitude, acceptance, forgiveness, and trust/patience.

2. We were born with love but we have learned fear which is the greatest impediment to love.

3. Our natural preference is to be safe, maintain the status quo, and resist both growth and love.

4. Love or fear, the choice is ours but if we remain passive and powerless in the face of perpetual opportunity, courage will help us progress.

5. It is better to be loving than right.

6. If we accept that we are loveable we will find that in all our interactions we are loved.

7. Truly loving requires a level of emotional development where we no longer fear caring for others more than caring for ourselves.

8. Self-love is critical; we can't give what we don't have.

9. Control obliterates love.

10. Judgment and comparison impede love.

11. Wisdom accentuates love and love embellishes wisdom. They create a dance of mutual reciprocity.

12. As with all the transformative spiritual tools, the consumer culture obstructs, hinders, and ultimately prevents the full development of love and wisdom.

13. In the spiritual realm there is only one dichotomy. All humans are from the same source and are one. All positive emotions are reflections of love while all negative emotions are reflections of fear.

14. The main purpose of fear is to keep us isolated and stagnant.

15. Fear is manifested in many ways. Anger, abuse, judgment, and addiction are just a few examples.

16. Fear and rage are the primary expressions of the child-self.

17. Each day, with every interaction we must intend to respond with love and caring. We have to see ourselves as manifestations of our higher power. In this way, we will achieve a life of contentment.

Chapter 11

Wisdom
Knowing That You Don't Know

"There are two things to aim at in life; first get what you want and after that enjoy it. Only the wisest of mankind achieve the second."
(Langdon Smith, 1901).

I. General Nature of Wisdom

"Wisdom is a virtue that pervades the universe and is innate within each of us." (Lama Surya Das, 2007).

A. Definition

"...but you will come to me tomorrow morning, I will stuff your head with brains. I cannot tell you how to use them, however; you must find that out for yourself." (The Wizard of Oz, 1900).

According to <u>The Random House Webster's Dictionary</u> (Fourth Edition, 2001) "wisdom" is "1. Scholarly knowledge or learning" while "wise" means "1. Having or showing disconcertment and good judgment"; "2. Having or showing scholarly language or learning; erudite" and "3. Knowing; informed." Yet for many spiritual scholars wisdom means seeing the "big picture" with compassion. Some Native American elders differentiate knowledge and wisdom believing that the former is about the present while the latter is about the future. Albert Einstein lamented that modern educational methods placed greater value on learning facts than developing and cultivating wisdom. T.S. Elliot concurs: "Where is the wisdom we have lost on knowledge." Don Miguel Ruiz (2004) writes: "Common sense is wisdom, and wisdom is different from knowledge. You are wise when you no longer act against yourself. You are wise when you live in harmony with yourself and with all of creation." On the other hand, the Talmud associates and defines wisdom as kindness. "Some theists say that wisdom is found while loving God while others maintain that wisdom is oneness and unity in vision." (Das, 2007). This author, defines wisdom as experience viewed from lenses of love and compassion.

B. Beyond the Dictionary

"But I do not want people to call me a fool, and if my head stays stuffed with straw instead of brains, as yours is, how am I ever to know anything?" (Scarecrow, The Wizard of Oz, 1900).

Although wisdom appears to mean a variety of things depending on one's perspective, it seems to be universally agreed that wisdom is a transformative quality to which all should aspire. It is unique among the traits previously mentioned here in that wisdom is dominated by life experience and contains a culmination of interdependent traits which can be comprehended when young but must be nurtured and honed throughout life. It is also agreed that wisdom connotes a peaceful and contented approach to existence which extends beyond self-interest and accepts a more inclusive view of cause and effect. Therefore wisdom seems to consist of a fluid combination of humility, gratitude, acceptance/forgiveness and trust/patience. All of these qualities of self-mastery are interdependent and equally necessary in wisdom's development. Each flows into and fortifies the other in a cycle of reciprocal reinforcement. They are inseparable; each is necessary for the utilization of the other yet stands unique in its contribution to the whole. With courage, wisdom becomes the intellectual expression and manifestation of love just as love becomes the preeminent emotional expression of wisdom.

C. <u>Wisdom is ubiquitous and unrestricted</u>

"The perfection of wisdom and the end of true philosophy is to proportion our wants to our possessions, our ambitions to our capacities, we will then be a happy and virtuous people."
(Mark Twain, 1835-1910).

The synergism of experience, love and courage results in wisdom. Wisdom knows when to go forward and when to retreat, what to include and what to omit, what we control and what we do not. Wisdom knows that it does not know all. It steps back, stays far from the crowd and considers. Wisdom is a process, a willingness to change and grow, to experience novel panoramas and perspectives. It has the courage to scrutinize. Wisdom bows and says: "teach me." It is harmony with the self and realizing that repeating the same mistakes leads to the same results. Wisdom also includes patience and trust. Like love it is generated from humility and shares acceptance. The wise see wisdom in all things and understand that they've just begun to learn.

II. Wisdom and Daily Living

"Within each experience of pain or negativity is the opportunity to challenge the perception that lies behind it, and to choose to learn with wisdom." (Gary Zukov, The Seat of the Soul, 1999).

A. The daily pursuit of wisdom (self-mastery)

"It is such an uncomfortable feeling to know one is a fool."
(Scarecrow, The Wizard of Oz, 1900).

Each day with each interaction we must strive to overpower the perspective of the personal and immediate in order to perceive a situation as it affects others and the future. We must consider the greater good and regulate our response based on attitudes of love, compassion, and understanding. This requires substantial reorientation of a world view from "how can I maximize personal rewards" to "how may I serve?"

Wisdom assists in this reconditioning by substituting unity for division, acceptance for rejection, gratitude for arrogance and trust for fear. This requires intent, awareness, perseverance, and self-control. Living in contentment necessitates diligent dedication to justice, harmony and truth. "It is impossible to live pleasurably without living wisely, well and justly." (Epicurus, 341-240 BCE).

"Wisdom is being able to see beyond the activities of the personality to the force of the immortal soul" as Gary Zukov writes in The Seat of the Soul (1999). "It is being able to see the role of responsible choice and choosing accordingly in each moment." Such focus and concentration creates a lucidity in thought which ". . . allows you to experience fellow humans with compassion instead of with judgment." "It allows the energy of the heart to flow." We begin to see beyond the obvious and into the spiritual.

Transgression diminishes with such wisdom and self-mastery because we are able to channel and constrain impulsive responses. Instead of panic, we distance, objectify and assess, thereby emphasizing self-control. Tension is put in perspective and becomes more tolerable. Mundane problems and their accompanying angst become framed as opportunities for growth. "Pain is only weakness leaving the body" say the Marines. Wisdom gives meaning to our lives and interactions because it lifts us beyond self-involvement. We become more than we would be otherwise. As Lama Surya Das (2007) writes: "Wise people internally understand how to regulate their emotions, body, and intellect. Sometimes wisdom consists of knowing what to focus on and what to ignore."

B. Wisdom and change

"What we cultivate in times of ease, we store up to support in times of change." (Buddah, C. 563-483 BCE).

"'I feel wise indeed' he answered earnestly. 'When I get used to my brains I shall know everything.'"
(Scarecrow, The Wizard of Oz, 1900).

One of the few certainties in life is change. As we become older, our perspective and life goals transform and we bend with reality. We feel our bodies lose the strength, endurance and flexibility they once had. We see our friends (those still with us and those who have passed on) differently, our objectives, jobs and world are all viewed through a different lens. With wisdom this transformation is met with compassion, acceptance, forgiveness and hopefully, humor.

Life and growth are change and change is stressful. It sometimes seems our innate disposition is to avoid this, to maintain the status quo, to remain in the womb. Transition can be an opportunity or it can be a source of significant anxiety. It is our choice and the wonder of wisdom is that one of its primary purposes is to guide us through turbulence towards contentment.

The stress that accompanies adjustment affects us in multiple areas. Frequently, the first feeling is vulnerability because we lack control. We may panic and wonder how this will pass. We may doubt our ability to be master of our fate and captain of our ship. However, wisdom will remind us that the external can always be controlled by the internal. To be aware, to see the larger picture, to stay in the moment are strategies of the wise and empowered. Acceptance, patience, and trust are tools which combine with wisdom to encourage growth and to navigate through the pain. The wise person understands that change is not to be feared rather it is the routine and unvarying which will destroy us. Therefore change is something that must be embraced and encouraged.

This is why it is critical to be aware of each moment and every interaction. No matter how trivial the thought, emotion, or event seems to be, awareness will pay great dividends both in the present and the future. "Blessed is the man who finds wisdom, who gains understanding; for he is more profitable than silver and yields better returns than gold." (Proverbs 3:13). Every moment of every day presents an occasion to give and express love, kindness, and compassion. This is how we live a contented life. Wisdom is the intellectual control center, but it is only effective when it channels love and humility to achieve acceptance of self, others and current circumstances. There is no wisdom without love and no love without wisdom.

C. <u>Self-Acceptance</u>

". . . but you may come with me, if you like. If Oz will not give you any brains you will be no worse off than you are now."
(<u>The Wizard of Oz</u>, 1900).

"Knowing others is knowledge. Knowing oneself is wisdom."
(Lao Tzu, 6th century BCE).

Accepting ourselves is a necessary condition for contentment. This is different from complacency which can be self-destructive as we marinate in self-satisfaction. Instead, self-acceptance is an attitude of treasuring ourselves because we honor our Source and our role in participating in the growth of all. Wisdom facilitates this process and promotes an embracing world view. Wisdom reminds us that ". . . everything we do affects all that lives and that our own seemingly individual existence is inextricably linked with countless other lives," writes Surya Das (2007). "We must become the wise ones and the visionary leaders we wish to see in the world today."

Wisdom and self-acceptance are also reciprocally related. Evolving as loving beings, self-acceptance emanates into a world view encompassing others and trusting the wisdom of the life force. A calmness and contentment begins to pervade the self and any defensiveness is defused. The need to judge yourself and others is mitigated, as wisdom and love determine a comprehensive perspective. The submissive urge for praise and the active avoidance of responsibility dissipate as we encounter challenges and changes. "As a rock remains unmoved by a storm, so the wise man remains unmoved by praise or blame." (The Dhammapada). "You no longer have the need to be good enough for anybody including yourself," Don Miguel Ruiz writes in Voice of Knowledge (2004), "You can accept what you are, whatever you are. . ."

D. Service to others

"What wisdom can you find that is greater than kindness."
(J.J. Rosseau, 1747).

"If I can stop one heart from breaking, I shall not live in vain."
(Emily Dickinson, 1865).

To be wise is to seek peace and contentment, to contemplate the moment and to intend compassion. It is to detach from the demands of the child-self in order to serve all persons. It is inclusion, love, and nurturance even as the child-self cries exclude, hate, and attack. Wisdom knows that happiness is supporting and assisting another. This is our purpose, our destiny. We are one with all and any person can keep us on wisdom's path.

We must develop wisdom in order to become all that is possible. Wisdom accesses and utilizes our fortitude and sensitivity. It "...motivates us to actualize our finest and truest self so that we can repeatedly actualize dynamic wisdom-moment after moment, crisis after crisis, opportunity after opportunity." (Lama Surya Das, 2007).

When we begin to focus on others and ask "how may I help?" rather than "what can I get?" we break the child-self cycle of narcissistic obsession. Our lives are no longer filled with what we do not need. We become empowered, effective, and generous. But we can never give more than we get. We must transform into more spiritual beings, emptying and discarding self-interest. We become filled with the love and spirit of others as we acquire wisdom and contentment. "Just as a bird with unfledged wings cannot fly up into the sky, so without the power of wisdom we cannot work for the good of others." (Atisa, 982-1053 ACE). The Dalai Lama (1998) agrees: "Human beings will have to develop a greater sense of universal responsibility. Each of us must learn to work not just for his or her own self, family or nation, but for the benefit of all mankind."

III. Wisdom, Synergy, and Contentment

"'Can't you give me your brains?' asked the Scarecrow.

'You don't need them. You are learning something everyday...
Experience is the only thing that brings knowledge, and the longer
you are on earth the more experience you are sure to get.'"
(Oz to the Scarecrow, The Wizard of Oz, 1900).

Wisdom is the highest form of knowledge and intelligence because it is the culmination of the interdependent interactions between and among humility, gratitude, acceptance/forgiveness and trust/patience. Wisdom and love are inseparable. With each and every activity, thought, and emotion the spiritually evolved person living a life of contentment will fuse these two characteristics. The proportions and dynamics will change according to circumstance but the totality will remain. Love and wisdom, wisdom and love will saturate our perspective and dominate our decision making.

A. **Wisdom and acceptance**

Wisdom blends each spiritual faculty into an essential world view that emanates an aura of love and acceptance. Wisdom is having the patience to realize that events occur at times during which we have no control. The planted seed will grow at a pace and result in characteristics dictated by nature and its own uniqueness, not based on our demand or desire. We have no effect on the outcome. To accept and acquiesce to this is to win the war against change. This is the only war winnable by raising a flag of surrender.

Wisdom is understanding and accepting that it is far better to be an observer than to be a manager. As Dr. Wayne Dyer points out you should:

> "Row, row, row, your boat,
> gently down the stream.
> Merrily, merrily, merrily,
> Life is but a dream."

"Go with the flow" and "ride the wave to the beach." Each cliché lauds the wisdom of acceptance.

Wisdom affirms the mundane because it knows there is a greater force at work. Wisdom is the result of experience as Oz tells the Scarecrow. Experience is the result of action and action involves judgment which involves choice. If we choose from a wise and loving perspective the result will always be beneficial. If we do not so choose we can at least learn, then grow and then advance. When we are wise, we embrace mistakes as opportunities to learn and move forward. Wisdom unifies the self through knowledge and acceptance. We cease being the "good" me or "bad" me and become "perfectly me." As Laurence Hope (1865-1904) writes: "For this is wisdom, to love, to live, to accept, and to take what fate, or the gods may give."

IV. Impediments

"The only problem is that our wisdom is obscured like a sun behind the clouds." (Tulku Thubten Rinpocher, 1980).

Wisdom is the pinnacle of intellectual development. Throughout the ages it has been sought precisely because it is so difficult to achieve. Attainment of wisdom is contingent upon rising above the ego child-self as well as achieving a perspective which blends the basic traits of transformation with selfless expressions of service and benevolence.

"Think about all the delusions, fantasies, misconceptions, and narrow points of view that pervade our own lives," writes Surya Das (2007). "Think about the ways in which we rationalize questionable behavior, engage in denial, and manipulate the truth not just with others but also with ourselves. Cultivating wisdom trains us away from these destructive habits of thinking, speaking, and behaving. It's a remedy for overcoming not only selfishness, stupidity and unfairness, but also feelings of confusion and meaninglessness." Indeed as we become genuine participant/observers in our life such consequences and rewards are realized.

A. Ignorance

"'It must be inconvenient to be made of flesh,' said the Scarecrow, thoughtfully, 'for you must sleep, and eat and drink. However, you have brains and it is worth a lot of bother to be able to think properly.'" (The Wizard of Oz, 1900).

Because we are unaware of its benefits and significance in achieving contentment, we do not pursue wisdom. Wisdom is both the cause and result of intellectual discipline and self-mastery. As we emerge from self-need to an expanded panorama we see, feel, behave and think differently. With courage driving us and moving us beyond ourselves, we begin to define our lives and our life goals with an altruistic perspective. We begin to regard the needs of others as important as our own. "Ignorance and delusion confine us and drive us into all kinds of craziness; misunderstanding and misconstruing things brings all kinds of problems. Wisdom is the answer, the antidote, the single medicine that relieves all ills and afflictions." (Das, 2007)

Wisdom facilitates objectivity and provides emotional control. We begin to frame mundane conflicts in magnanimous terms, as life's travails are prioritized and arranged into an appropriate perspective. From this springs a more spiritual, loving, accepting and understanding overview. We become "enlightened" as we let knowledge shine into our assumptions. Our lives and actions achieve meaning as we progress into awareness and altruism. "We have to know who we are and what is real in the world around us and in the light of this understanding, intuit what it is we truly want and need. Otherwise we have no hope of accomplishing or attaining anything worthwhile." (Surya Das, 2007).

B. Fear

"We're separated from our own reality by a veil of illusion, and within that illusion we feel great fear." (Williamson, 2004).

Once again fear and anxiety arise to impede progress and perception. This underscores the necessity and relevance of courage in our own pursuit of contentment. The child-self continually cries out that it is powerless to choose or behave differently. We desperately hold on to our delusions and misconceptions despite their destructiveness. The child demands, sameness, ritual and routine. "All is as it appears or else I'm doomed." Fear drives us into inaction, tunnel vision and bias. But fear can also be a motivation, an opportunity to change and grow; a chance to learn who we really are and to embrace our unique role in larger, grander, plan. Our goal is to turn fear and inaction into challenge, enemies into friends and hiding into confronting.

C. <u>Arrogance</u>

"From pride, vainglory, and hypocrisy;
from envy, hatred, and malice and all uncharitableness
Good Lord, deliver us."
(Book of Common Prayer).

Arrogance is another component of our child-self which impedes intelligence from evolving into wisdom, love, humility and genuine pride. Arrogance is pride polluted by the child-self. Pride is a natural and self-rewarding feeling of worth and efficacy which results from achievement. Arrogance, on the other hand, is a feeling of superiority and entitlement which completely annihilates the "we" for the "I."

Arrogance is a mark we wear to hide the fear of vulnerability and self-discovery. It restricts any attempt to defeat the forces of stagnation and self-satisfaction. If we are to strive for advancement we must face the unpleasant truth of our current situation. With humility and courage we can overpower the child-self and strive for wisdom. As T.S. Eliot writes: "The only wisdom we can hope to acquire is the wisdom of humility." (1940). To moderate this tendency of arrogance and complacency, the basic transformative tool of humility is necessary. With humility, which is the basis of all other life-enhancing ideals, arrogance is tempered. Humility reinforces the vital role wisdom plays in achieving contentment. With humility, we gain the courage and motivation to change, to face fear and move on.

D. Once again, culture

Our culture strongly discourages thinking, let alone wisdom. To be inarticulate and uninformed is to be "cool" and carefree. Advertising does not want us to think beyond the brief message presented on T.V. Many politicians believe that our attention span and comprehension do not extend past the space occupied by a bumper sticker. We are told what is wrong with us and how to fix it. No thought or reconsideration is necessary. How simple and effortless it is to passively go through life, certain, and secure in our misconceptions, complacent in our incomprehension.

It takes work, intent, and awareness to extricate ourselves from the swamp of this stupor. First of all, it takes the gift of enlightenment, of insight, and objectivity to see that there is a problem. Then it takes courage to identify it and motivation to construct a plan of attack. Indeed, acknowledging our feelings of discomfort with our present circumstances and accepting the responsibility for revision ("to see again") is a spiritual gift available to all. Wisdom and love are the transcendental connections to our source, the ultimate life force guiding the Universe. Dare to see and dare to aspire. Horace (65-8 BCE) gives us one more dare: "Dare to be wise; when you begin you are already halfway there."

V. Summary

"If you only had your brains in your head you would be as good a man as any of them...Brains are the only things worth having in this world, no matter whether one is a crow or a man."
(Crow to Scarecrow, The Wizard of Oz, 1900).

As humility, gratitude, acceptance/forgiveness and patience/trust grow and interact reciprocally, wisdom is created. This is a function of time, intent, awareness, and assimilated experience which explains why wisdom is not attained by many who are

232

nonetheless spiritually developed. Wisdom also requires an intermixture of understanding, love, and compassion such that they blend into a whole while retaining their individual flavors.

Wisdom is more than a simple accumulation of the basic transformative tools. Rather it is a seismic change of perspective which becomes permanently blended into our daily life. Wisdom is a goal, an achievement that requires a relinquishment of will. It is so much more than knowledge (accumulation of facts) and intelligence (the ability to incorporate and connect facts which results in a higher level of thinking and a more abstract conclusion). Wisdom is an all encompassing, inclusive perspective such that we perceive life from a unique mindset. It is the culmination of experience reviewed and comprehended with love and acceptance. Wisdom is courage because it is inclusion. It is acceptance because it does not manage, it observes. It is humility because it knows its boundaries and it is gratitude because it enhances spirit.

Wisdom is understanding and accepting what happens because we know it is part of a greater plan. It is a belief that the Universe and events are exactly as they should be. It is acceptance of the self and the "other" with the knowledge that God makes not mistakes.

When we fulfill our destiny and gain wisdom we also achieve contentment and self actualization. As love and wisdom are joined, they interact and influence all aspects of our lives so that positive change is inevitable for us and everyone we encounter. At this point all of our actions, thoughts, and feelings are suffused with each of the basic transformative qualities, directed by the head-heart combination and fueled by courage. We are at the peak of our functioning and at the epitome of physical and spiritual development. This is our goal and our destiny.

"Knowledge is proud that he has learned so much;
Wisdom is humble that he knows no more." (William Cow, 1785).

VI. For Further Consideration

1. For many spiritual scholars wisdom is more than knowledge and learning. It is seeing the "big picture."

2. The synergism of life experience, love, and humility results in wisdom.

3. Wisdom encompasses a sea-change in perspective from "What's in it for me?" to "How may I serve?"

4. Wisdom requires self-control and self-mastery. The intellect dominates but does not exclude the emotions.

5. Wisdom helps us cope with change so that the end result is growth and love.

6. Awareness and intent are necessary qualities in the quest for wisdom.

7. Evolving as a loving spirit is the cause and result of self-acceptance which in turn blossoms into a world-view embracing others and trusting in a plan greater than ourselves. This is one aspect of wisdom.

8. Judgment and comparison cease to exist when love and wisdom dominate our perspective.

9. Wisdom knows that true happiness lies in service to others.

10. Wisdom is the highest form of knowledge and intelligence. It is the culmination of the reciprocal interactions between and among all the basic transformative attributes which lead to self-actualization.

11. Wisdom blends each spiritual faculty into a fundamental perspective that generates an aura of love and acceptance.

12. If we choose and behave from a perspective of wisdom and love the results will always be beneficial.

13. Wisdom is prone to the same impediments that plague all growth such as ignorance, fear, arrogance, and the culture of consumption.

<u>Remember!!</u>

"We do not receive wisdom, we must discover it for ourselves, after a long journey through the wilderness which no one else can make for us, for our wisdom is the point of view from which we come at last to regard the world." (Marcel Proust, 1871-1922).

Chapter 12

The Fear of Courage

"Then, if you don't mind, I'll go with you," said the Lion,
"for my life is simply unbearable without a bit of courage."
(Lion to Dorothy, The Wizard of Oz, 1900).

I. The General Nature of Courage

A. Definition

"There is no living thing that is not afraid when it faces danger.
True courage is in facing danger when you are afraid and that kind
of courage you have plenty." (Oz to Lion, The Wizard of Oz, 1900).

The American Heritage Dictionary (Fourth Edition, 2001) defines "courage" as: "The quality of mind that enables one to face danger with self possession, confidence and resolution; bravery." According to The Oxford American Dictionary 1980, "courage" means: "The ability to control fear when facing danger or pain, bravery." Common synonyms for "courage" include: "audacity," "daring," "determination," "fortitude," and "tenacity." The word "courage" once referred to the heart as the seat of feelings. It is from Old French "corage" and from Latin "cor" "heart." (The Oxford Dictionary of Word Histories, 2002).

B. <u>Courage and humility</u>

What is the nature of courage and how is it related to humility? At first glance courage appears to be the polar opposite of humility. If this is the case, how could one strive to expand humility and courage when they conflict with each other? To achieve growth and fulfillment both must become basic components of our personality and life perspective. If they cancel each other out, focusing on their development would be a fool's errand.

Courage frequently connotes actions such as slaying a lion, confronting an abuser or some other kind of aggressive, self-protective act in defense of the physical self. Humility, on the other hand, connotes subservience, meekness and passivity. Yet, does not the Bible say; "Turn the other cheek"? Was Gandhi not courageous as he passively conquered the British Empire without aggression? Was not Martin Luther King courageous as he passively and humbly resisted the forces of hate and anger? Were not both of these intrepid men humble and empowered?

Courage requires both internal (emotional) and external (behavioral) components. Courage is as much moral fortitude as bravery, as much the ability to walk away as to confront, as much spiritual as physical. Courage incorporates and expresses humility by surrendering and having the strength to be vulnerable. It takes as much courage to accept assets of character as it does deficits. Courage is necessary to accept God's plan and to embrace those aspects we control and to let go of those we can't.

Courage is a necessary factor in our spiritual, emotional and behavioral quest for growth and contentment. It both empowers and humbles. If we are to succeed we must have the courage and humility to let go of our past and embrace all that we can be. As George Elliot wrote, "It is never too late to be what you might have been."

II. Courage in Daily Life

"Courage is to feel the daily daggers of relentless steel and keep on living." (Douglas Mallock, 1877 – 1938).

A. The challenge of courage

"Courage is the price that life exacts for granting peace." (Amelia Earhart, 1932).

In order to achieve wellness, freedom and growth, courage must permeate all aspects of your life. You need courage to be humble, grateful, patient, accepting, wise and loving. To have the courage to be happy, to take risks in the interest of evolving and expanding, to cherish ourselves and those around us, to teach and to learn are the goals of a well-lived life. To make your unique contribution and to participate in life according to principles and beliefs based on love and acceptance is to exhibit courage.

Such principles rely on trust in a plan greater than ourselves devised by a beneficent power whose goodness and wisdom are beyond imagination. Be humble and learn. Watch and listen. God speaks. Thucydides (431 BCE) wrote: "…the secret to happiness is freedom and the secret to freedom is courage."

Show courage; take responsibility for your life and your choices. Have the courage to be you. There is no greater gift. As you free yourself from the good and bad opinion of others, you begin to mold life as it is meant to be lived. "We are being challenged by world events, by the tides of history, to develop a more mature consciousness," writes Marianne Williamson in The Gift of Change (2004). "Yet we cannot do this without facing what hurts."

B. The origins of courage

"You have plenty of courage, I am sure," answered Oz. "All you need is confidence in yourself." (The Wizard of Oz, 1990).

Where does courage come from? How do we rise up to have the motivation and confidence to confront that which we've always avoided, excused, rationalized, or dismissed? The answer is that it comes from patience as well as trust in the goodness of the universe and in the self confidence that we are becoming who we were meant to be. As Marianne Williamson writes (2004): "You gain strength, courage and confidence by every experience in which you really stop to look fear in the face. You are able to say to yourself, 'I lived through this horror. I can take the next thing that comes along.'" Writes Eleanor Roosevelt (1949) "You must do the thing you think you cannot do."

C. Courage and thought

"But my people have worn green glasses on their eyes so long that most of them think it really is an Emerald City."
(The Wizard of Oz, 1900).

In order to become empowered and to take responsibility for our life, we must first take responsibility for our thoughts. With awareness and intent we will better monitor our thoughts and receive the appropriate signal, in spite of superficial noise. The Serenity Prayer states that we must have the courage to change that which we can control. With each reaction and interaction, if we so choose, we can control our thoughts, behavior and feelings. Furthermore, as we progress from the "I" (self-centered thought) to the "we" ("other" centered thought) we begin to accept our inability to control most events, including the behavior of others. Surrender your arrogance and fear so as to accept this fact with courage. Our intrinsic control is how we react to that which happens and how we interpret that reaction as it defines who we are.

D. <u>Courage and awareness</u>

"Courage means facing what we can't change."
(<u>Keep It Simple</u>, Hazelton, 1989).

Our destiny is to be on a path that allows life to be filled with contentment but we must first focus on this goal and cultivate our awareness of the cues that point to the right course. With awareness we can control our thoughts. Awareness provides us with a moment of reflection to pause and better evaluate our actions, thereby preventing impulsive acting out. Intention is the motivation to achieve while awareness provides the perspective to attainment. Awareness spots the signals that steer success.

Courage supplies awareness when we are moving too close to "group think" and farther away from our core beliefs, perspectives and goals. It gives us the strength to be a majority of one in any crowd. With courage and awareness we see both our weakness and our strength. We free ourselves from the burden of who we are supposed to be and how we are supposed to act based on past mythical beliefs. We become able to be vulnerable and face truth without fear of censure. Courage strengthens us to see and share our imperfections as we learn and mature.

Such awareness changes our perceptions and as we change perceptions we change behavior and our very essence. We now know what we should do in order to be who we were destined to be. When we learn these things our lives become purposeful and each act, thought and emotion are unique contributions to a grand plan.

E. <u>Courage and problem solving</u>

"...before she had time to think about it, she was safe on the other side." (<u>The Wizard of Oz</u>, 1900).

"Courage and perseverance have a magical talisman, before which difficulties disappear and obstacles vanish into air." (John Quincy Adams, 1805).

The virtue of courage is a crucial component throughout the problem solving process and effective problem solving is essential if one is to learn and grow. Frequently, identifying and articulating discomfort, distress or malaise is in itself a generator of productive living because we would rather ignore pain than face it. So the first step in problem solving is to eviscerate any denial and to refocus on our goal of internal wellness. Once we accept the fact that all is not well and that we have the responsibility to remedy the situation we may begin to determine the core issues and subsequently formulate a productive plan.

F. <u>Denial</u>

Denial becomes an obstacle to success because it renounces responsibility for creating and solving a problem. Frequently, denial will ignore a problem as though it did not exist. Denial also obfuscates and obscures the wide variety of solutions which are available. When fear and distrust hinder perspective, we tend to myopically repeat past behaviors, despite experience. Consequently, we luxuriate in the status quo. Courage will pierce this self-destructive delusion so that we may honestly determine the problem and pursue a different, more fulfilling resolution. As we persevere, appraise and assess, courage will enable us to concentrate on our intent and purpose. The self-indulgent distortions that would divert us from a successful conclusion and allow us to reassess results will be minimized. If necessary, we can modify the plan and continue efforts towards a resolution.

241

Consequently, courage plays a significant role in each stage of problem solving by dissolving the defense mechanism of denial and allowing us to face both the fear of change and the self-deception that minimal effort creates maximum results. Courage is a fundamental temperament that inspires action in all areas of living. It is indispensable for the expression of each spiritual quality that constitutes a life of serenity.

G. Courage in daily life

"...now I am anxious for a chance to show the other beasts how courageous I have grown." (The Wizard of Oz, 1900).

Courage is a prerequisite quality if we are to continue on our spiritual path to fulfillment. It is as crucial to the smaller scale of daily living as it is to the grand plan of our destiny. Courage gives us options in life and living. It inspires us to move in directions that we were meant to pursue. It emboldens us to face self-deceit and delusion while giving us the freedom to act in a manner independent of external pressures. Courage assists us in the challenge of self-discovery and effective problem solving. It empowers us to face daily hurdles with love and acceptance. Most importantly, courage arouses and galvanizes us to play the hand we are given with love, competence and acceptance.

III. Courage and Our Ultimate Destiny

"Courage is reckoned the greatest of all virtues because unless a man has that virtue, he has no security for preserving any other." (Samuel Johnson, 1709-1784).

Courage is the behavioral expression and emotional conduit to the ultimate goal of living in wisdom and love. While courage is the underpinning of all the spiritual characteristics to which we aspire (humility, gratitude, acceptance, patience, etc.) it is especially important as we begin to develop into the next stratum of self-actualization. This is our transcendental goal so that all interactions, thoughts, behaviors, and feelings are grounded in love and wisdom while manifested through courage. It is here that acceptance is the rule and rejection the exception. The "I" subserves the "we" as the "they" and the "them" diminish to the point of near imperceptibility. It is in this space that we live as we were meant to and it is here where we realize our destiny. Courage is the catalyst which makes this materialize.

A. The many facets of courage

"I haven't the heart to harm even a Witch' remarked the Tin Woodman, 'but you if you go I shall certainly go with you.'"
(The Wizard of Oz, 1900).

Honesty requires the courage to see yourself as others see you, both vices and virtues. We need to learn from others, to be open to their perspectives without the coercion of conformity. This is the function of the participant/observer. Such boldness motivates you to separate faults and strengths from the myths that are your life story. Courage is to discover, to experiment and to learn how to be you. It is to understand who you are and your role in this life. It gives you the incentive and vigor to pursue your passion. It is the capacity to recreate, to rise above and reassemble the pieces so at to move forward on an unfamiliar path using new strategies. Courage is the empowerment of independence. It is necessary for our growth and evolution.

In short, courage helps us reach a new dimension in development and spirituality by (1) freeing us from both the good and bad opinions of others; (2) more clearly defining us as we meet challenges; (3) allowing us to fail; (4) enhancing our journey of self-discovery as we embrace and assimilate humility, gratitude, acceptance/forgiveness and trust/patience; and (5) fortifying us to face truth.

Marianne Williamson (2004) writes that the spiritual meaning of every situation is not what happens to us but what we do with what happens to us and who we decide to become. "The only real failure is the failure to grow from what we go through" she notes and the main obstacle to growth is the false security we get from the status-quo. We blithely stagnate because we don't want to face the disruption that accompanies change. Courage will change that.

B. <u>Courage and "The Grand Plan"</u>

"Behind them was the dark forest they had passed safely through,
although they had suffered many discouragements; but before them
was a lovely, sunny country that seemed to beckon them
on to the Emerald City." (<u>The Wizard of Oz</u>, 1900).

Courage is the ultimate expression of the "life force." It rises to proclaim life and love as the proven powers of the universe. It has the fortitude to support and cherish the downtrodden, to defend the weak, and to oppose the popular. Courage is the quality that allows us to cope with life as we use our spiritual perspective to nurture and reinforce humility, gratitude, acceptance and patience. Courage allows us to affirm the changeless and to change the changeable. It provides the energy to incite and revitalize the spiritual qualities necessary to function effectively and to achieve fulfillment.

To have courage is to have contentment because we live without fear. Either you will succeed, that is meet your expectations by achieving your goal, or you will not. Courage, patience/trust and humility help us accept that this is a process and not a destination. Every ending is the parent of a beginning. Courage reminds us that what lies ahead is what is meant to be and that you will learn and grow as you confront challenges. Your mantra becomes: "I am one of many, I am small and I am large, my job, my fate is to be both as perfect as I can be and as imperfect as I am. I must love, accept, learn and progress in order to create the me I am meant to be." There is no greater challenge, nor greater reward and courage is a necessary condition to achieve this state.

IV. Impediments

A. The origin of courage

"Whatever you do, you need courage. Whatever course you decide upon, there is always someone to tell you that you are wrong."
(Ralph Waldo Emerson, 1803-1882).

In our daily lives, obstacles abound as we attempt to assimilate courage with wisdom and love. Developing courage is impeded by the usual demons of culture, fear, apathy, and low self-esteem. If it takes courage to create courage how do we begin?

Basically, courage is generated by the very fear that first attempts to suppress it through denial and complacency. Courage appears when all other options are exhausted. We are at our bottom when we have no alternatives but those which have been steadfastly resisted, namely growth and maturity. When we have finally failed in our efforts to maintain the status quo, to remain stuck, to blame every possible outside force, we must look inside, take responsibility and act. It is then that courage appears. Sometimes events foment growth and development. Despite deeply ingrained beliefs that we are incapable of change, helpless in the face of outside forces and inescapably reliant on others, we find that we must decide and we must adapt. We see no choice, it is do or die. It is then that courage is born.

As Marianne Williamson (2004) writes, "...we are subtly and insidiously convinced that our natural powers do not exist. We become slaves to a world view in which our human powers are diminished, seen as secondary to the astonishing powers of science technology and other false goals of the external planes.

Modern progress seems to overrule our souls, leaving us bereft within a meaningless universe." These beliefs must be identified, challenged, and subjugated. Courage is necessary to succeed in all these areas. As it serves to force us to face fear, so too it grows more resolute from this battle as it builds our self-esteem. "What doesn't destroy us, makes us stronger." (Nietzche, 1844-1900).

B. Low self-esteem

"'I will go too,' declared the Scarecrow; 'but I shall not be of much help to you, I am such a fool.'" (The Wizard of Oz, 1900).

"Courage is resistance to fear, mastery of fear – not absence of fear." (Mark Twain, 1894).

Low self-esteem is basically a deeply ingrained, incorrect and self-destructive belief that we are either incapable or unworthy of self-fulfillment. The idea of empowerment fills us with dread as we remember the multiple failures of our past. We would prefer to retain the demeaning, insulting and debilitating circumstances of present existence than to go on a path of independence and discovery. We have accepted and submitted to helplessness. "We" are small, defective and debilitated; "they" are intelligent, attractive, strong and confident. "They" have the answer.

This has been decided for us before we discovered who we are and what we can do. We've frequently been taught to focus on what we are not and where we are inadequate rather than who we are and where we are powerful. We are haunted by our mistakes and oblivious of our successes. "Rather than being helped to understand how we best function, how to find the solution that works best for us, we have become a people who look to define who we should be, how we should feel and how we should live. This has led to an increased incapacity to deal with life." (Williamson, 2004). It takes more courage to be introspective and see our power than to marinate in dependency and debility. Success is often more frightening than failure.

V. Summary

"Often the test of courage is not to die but to live."
(Vittorio Alfieri).

In conclusion, courage is the ability to live positively. We set about accentuating affirmative thoughts regarding ourselves, others, and our world. Hence, boundaries become more permeable as we effortlessly feel empathy and compassion. The "I" slowly evolves into the "we" as the "them" gradually diminishes.

With courage we begin to take responsibility for our essential goodness. We learn to embrace and cherish ourselves because there is a reason and purpose to our existence. Courage reveals that purpose and motivates us to fulfill our destiny. With courage we will always do our best because we fear neither failure nor criticism. "Success is going from failure to failure without loss of enthusiasm", Winston Churchill famously said. This is the essence of courage especially if combined with patience and trust. We realize that there is no real defeat, only an occasion to learn. As Thomas Edison believed, when things don't go our way it's not that we're unsuccessful, rather we have been successful in learning what doesn't work.

Courage empowers us to live as we were created to live; to make a difference, accomplish and progress according to a transcendent spiritual plan. With courage we abandon the ego/child-self to trust in this delicate design. We now develop the patience to accept and become participant-observers during detours, blockades and assorted frustrations. Without courage we cannot experience freedom or love. We cannot realize our destiny.

When we become infused with courage, trust, love, acceptance and contentment are created. The perfect ceases to impede the good. We strive to do our best and we feel satisfied when we complete our task. We no longer have to become more than we are. We learn to be. "Crossing the bridge to a better world begins with crossing a bridge inside our minds from the addictive mental patterns of fear and separation to an enlightened perception of unity and love." (Marianne Williamson, 2004).

VI. For Further Consideration

1. Courage has many meanings, well beyond the simple meaning of the ability to face external danger.

2. Courage both empowers and humbles. Humility and courage are in a reciprocal relationship, each reinforces the other.

3. Courage is necessary for fulfillment because it motivates us to persevere.

4. Courage allows us to discover and accept our true nature.

5. We must have courage if we are to participate in and contribute to life.

6. Freedom is a necessary component of happiness and courage is necessary for freedom.

7. Courage is spawned by conflict, pain and desperation.

8. With courage we learn to control what we can, namely our thoughts, feelings and behavior.

9. Courage sharpens and encourages our awareness of the truths that surround us.

10. Courage liberates us from both the good and bad opinion of others.

11. Courage enables us to more effectively and efficiently evaluate and resolve daily dilemmas.

12. Courage rouses us to action based on our newfound beliefs. Therefore, we learn and advance.

13. Courage enhances our life perspective, thereby expanding our options.

14. Courage is the behavioral expression and the emotional conduit to the ultimate goal of living in wisdom and love.

15. Courage creates compassion and empathy by diminishing the "I" in favor of the "we" and "us."

16. Courage is the preeminent expression of our "life force."

17. Courage is naturally impeded by the usual demons of culture, fear, apathy and low self-esteem.

Part V

Beginning Again

"'Where is Kansas?' asked the man, with surprise.

'I don't know,' replied Dorothy sorrowfully, 'but it is my home, and I'm sure it's somewhere.'"

(The Wizard of Oz, 1900).

"The Scarecrow and the Tin Woodman and the Lion now thanked the Good Witch earnestly for her kindness, and Dorothy exclaimed: 'You are certainly as good as you are beautiful! But you have not yet told me how to get back to Kansas.'"

"'Your silver shoes will carry you over the desert,' replied Glinda. 'If you had known their power you could have gone back to Aunt Em the very first day you come to this country.'"

(The Wizard of Oz, 1900).

Bringing It All Together

It is now time to use the lessons of the past to take control and shape the future. You need to create a plan so that you avoid the glitz and seduction of a yellow brick road and choose a personal path forged by love and compassion. Your Personal Development Program will serve as anchor and guide, testament and signpost.

As Dorothy struggled to discover herself and find her home, we too must be challenged by change and turmoil in order to evolve and grow. The process of trial and error requires ascertaining strengths and weaknesses while manifesting both mastery and incompetence. Simultaneously, we learn control and surrender, courage and humility, wisdom and bewilderment. While the end merges into the beginning and the process progresses, the journey evolves and gains in significance and singularity. Now, we must be introspective and re-establish our goals as we act with loving intent and optimistic awareness. Compassion and contentment will prevail as we pursue our destiny and transform our very being. With a Personal Development Program we create a map to help navigate an uncharted future and produce the person we were meant to be.

Chapter 13

The Personal Development Program
Mapping the Journey

*". . . they did not dare change the direction of their journey
for fear of getting lost." (<u>The Wizard of Oz</u>, 1900).*

I. Purpose

*". . . no one who learns to know himself remains just what
he was before." (Thomas Mann, 1875-1955).*

If you were to begin a journey into the unknown it would
be natural to plan in advance, consult previous travelers, obtain
a map etc. The Personal Development Program (PDP) is your
map. Its purpose is to provide a path and give direction. If you
are to get the most benefit from this book, it is essential that
you complete all the steps necessary to create a PDP. The intent
of the PDP is to delineate and focus on goals as a commitment
to a course of action. The PDP is a tool, a very valuable and
effective tool, that will reprogram thinking and thereby point

your behavior in a direction of self-fulfillment. By using this tool you will more readily achieve love, acceptance, courage and ultimately, contentment.

A. Defining the vague

When constructing a Personal Development Program you begin to develop and objectify the vague and indeterminate aspects of your fantasy, imagination and goals. As your pen glides over the paper, these amorphous, nonverbalized ambitions are given form and substance. You are generating awareness and intent as you struggle to verbalize and articulate your dreams and desires. The combination of the fanciful with the practical can provide an energy and dynamic which will facilitate action. You will uncover hidden aspects of your personality and find patterns in external events previously unknown and unrecognized.

The PDP produces a unique opportunity to focus, plan, set goals, reassess, re-evaluate, reset goals and change course as we experience the learning process of trial and error. The long-term PDP contributes support during change and chaos. It is a commitment to specific principles and ways of behaving. The long-term PDP rarely changes because it reflects our ideal self, the self to which we aspire. The short-term PDP will change gradually over time as we adapt to the whims of the world as well as the effects of behavior in the pursuit of objectives.

All major religions have rites and rituals wherein the adherents regularly refocus and reflect on the primary aspirations which relate to current behavior. The purpose of such reflection is to determine if the ideal self is consistent with routine conduct as we attempt to accomplish life's mission. The degree to which our behavior is ineffective or disparate from our ideal self is the degree to which we are subject to depression, anxiety and low self-esteem. So it is critical that we are introspective and monitor our progress as often as possible. As you write, you essentially learn what you think and in so doing, you recreate the self and the person you strive to be.

256

B. Self-evaluation

"'I'm supposed to be a Great Wizard.' 'And aren't you?' she asked.
'Not a bit of it, my dear; I'm just a common man.'"
<u>*The Wizard of Oz*</u>, *1900).*

The ultimate goal of the Personal Development Program is to create a method of self-evaluation and progress that assesses the cultivation of humility, gratitude, acceptance, patience, courage, wisdom and love in our daily lives. As we advance in this quest of self-evaluation we benefit ourselves and those around us. The PDP is a continual confrontation with the self facilitating the role of participant/observer as we respond to the challenge of daily living. With this method we recall all new learning experiences while we simultaneously compare our inner wishes with the actual experiences. As such, we begin to discover creative solutions to internal conflicts.

C. Empowerment

"The Tin Woodman knew very well he had no heart, and therefore
he took great care never to be cruel or unkind to anything."
<u>*The Wizard of Oz*</u>, *1900).*

Life in general and change in particular are more stressful when you feel powerless. By referring to and writing a PDP, you get a sense of control and mastery. Through this writing you create and implement a plan designed to manage stress and achieve goals. Every time you achieve a goal it is noted as well as the strategy used. In this way you increase the skill set for meeting and mastering ever diverse demands. Like an architect adapting an abstract concept of the perfect house to a concrete, practical plan, the PDP will transform the ideal into the real. You will begin to visualize and design the person you had always hoped to be.

In sum, as you formulate a PDP, you begin to recreate your life. In essence, you are focusing on specific goals to be achieved in a manner consistent with your ideal self. You will fall short because an ideal, by its nature, cannot be perfectly achieved. But don't let the exemplary prevent you from trying. The PDP can help identify patterns of behavior that are self-defeating and destructive, as well as life affirming and productive. Furthermore, it gives clarity to chaos and resolve to doubt. You begin to develop a different identity which includes a sense of mastery and self-acceptance. In short, the PDP can give you a focus and compass as it coalesces past lessons with future goals in a present plan.

II. Advantages

"Dorothy did not know what to say to this, for all the people seemed to think her a witch, and she knew very well she was only an ordinary little girl who had come by the chance of a cyclone into a strange land." (The Wizard of Oz, 1900).

As you construct, review and revise the PDP, you will notice a significant change in your perspective. You will more clearly see the difference between effective and detrimental choices and your motivation and sense of empowerment will become palpable. This is an indication of how profoundly behavior patterns have altered. You may want to pause for a moment to reflect on the transformation of those around you and how your world, in general, has become more peaceful and loving.

A. The writing process

"It's not what you look at that matters, it's what you see." (Henry David Thoreau, 1817-1862).

As you write, be open, flexible, daring and imaginative. If you are afraid to put it on paper, it is a sure sign that you should. Writing will highlight new and pleasant characteristics of yourself which previously could have been reflexively dismissed as "not like you." You will develop a target, intention and awareness which will become evident in daily interactions, observations and assessments. Each day a clarity of purpose will guide you, giving the courage to risk, thereby facilitating success. The Personal Development Program allows you to safely express feelings and tensions. You will be able to articulate conflicts, mentally encounter them and formulate a plan of action before entering the arena.

With a PDP and the concentration it brings you will create clear analysis, concrete goals and effective decisions. It is a path to self-awareness and a means of achieving self-identity. In the midst of chaos, crisis and change, it erects a method to contentment, attainment and completion. The PDP is a means to gain insight into emotions and a mechanism to resolve past conflicts. The very act of putting pen to paper, in itself, is an affirmation and a commitment to change, progress and productivity. The decision to create a PDP leads to the deliberate and conscious act of writing. It is the first physical step towards self-actualization as body and mind unite to formulate the future.

B. The Personal Development Program and responsibility

"The naked truth of spiritual transformation is that if we don't change our lives ourselves, nothing will change them for us. That's the secret of spiritual self-mastery." (Lama Surya Das, 2007).

"'Oz, left to himself, smiled to think of his success in giving the Scarecrow and the Tin Woodman and the Lion exactly what they thought they wanted. 'How can I help being a humbug,' he said, 'when all these people make me do things that everybody knows can't be done?'" (The Wizard of Oz, 1900).

It is our responsibility to change and grow; to shed previous illusory perspectives about who we are and what we must do to satisfy our unique destiny. The PDP is an effective means of undertaking that responsibility and persevering on that journey. Through the PDP you can shape your perspective so that it is one of optimism, empowerment and success. As you become more aware of your world view, you become more sensitive to biases, distortions and preconceptions. What you note in the PDP will more likely be experienced in everyday living.

As you record your intention and commitment to achievement, the opportunity to manifest this is more easily found in your daily routine because self-expression sensitizes awareness. You discover causation where it never existed and find yourself surrounded by a bounty of possibility. This magnifies motivation, setting up a cycle of affirmative reciprocity. Intent and awareness transform internal ambitions into external events. As you write, you resolve and you create. You are limited only by imagination and fear of success. The PDP compels you to focus in times of change and turbulence. It is your personal bible and unique map to contentment. It provokes you to be both consistent in your resolve and flexible in your approach, open to change yet cautious of external and internal distractions and deceptions.

By means of the PDP, we give ourselves an opportunity to take advantage of a pause between impulse and action. We consider, discern and grow while maintaining a concentration on the ideal self and future goals. A PDP outlines our unique position in life and constructs a personal interpretation of our importance and function in the Grand Plan.

C. **Summary**

"The difficult is what takes a little time; the impossible is what takes a little longer." (Fridtjof Nansen, 1861-1930).

"Dorothy told the Witch all her story: how the cyclone had brought her to the Land of Oz, how she had found her companions, and of the wonderful adventures they had met with."
(The Wizard of Oz, 1900).

If we are to progress, secure contentment, extend respect and determine our destiny we need a plan consisting of general long-term goals as well as specific and malleable, short-term goals. Each day is filled with random events, constant and contradictory messages in addition to ceaseless references to the external, the immediate and the transitory. We live in a world of paralyzing noise and diminishing signal.

To find our way and stay the course we require a map which delineates needs from wants, ideals from practicality and the general from the specific. The PDP serves this purpose. It is essential if we are to shed the past, conquer dependency and vulnerability as well as forge ahead towards freedom and self-discovery.

III. Constructing the Foundation

"Yet the paradox always lingers . . . we are in control/we are not in control, doomed to make choices." (Wayne W. Dyer, 1998).

"If you had only known their power you could have gone back to your Aunt Em the very first day you came to this country."
(The Wizard of Oz, 1900).

We now understand that what we need is abundant in the here and now. It is always around us ready to be activated in the pursuit of our higher purpose. As you develop your intent and subsequent awareness, this will not seem so mystical. Rather you will accept it as truth. As we learn a new concept, sensation or impression, it begins to appear with ever more regularity into our daily consciousness. Similarly, when you write something down you affirm your commitment to creating it. You then begin to search for evidence that it is becoming manifested in your life and you behave in ways that facilitate this manifestation. Is this magic? Maybe. If magic is fulfilling your intention, then this is magic and we are endlessly encompassed by magic as we navigate our destiny.

The first step is believing and the second is acting. Always move forward as you modify behavior and thought. Act, assess, regroup and act again, always advancing, adapting and completing. In this way we mold ourselves and discover fulfillment. As such we create reality and begin to reinterpret our selves and the world with each new experience.

A. Choosing attitudes and beliefs

"At first she had wondered if she would be dashed to pieces when the house fell again; but as the hours past and nothing terrible happened, she stopped worrying and resolved to wait calmly and see what the future would bring." (The Wizard of Oz, 1900).

In order to compose a valid PDP we must choose certain attitudes and beliefs that will direct and frame our goals. We should also strive to truly know ourselves and to separate the practical from the perfect. Once we appreciate that we are the designers of a new self we have to take responsibility for how our choices affect others. If we focus on the development and nurturance of humility, gratitude, acceptance/forgiveness and patience/trust, altruism will determine our goals. To love is to be loved and to give is to receive. When we contemplate our future goals with the awareness that what we offer to another is returned exponentially, we begin to comprehend the limitless potential of joyful generosity.

B. Choice and change

"Do not fear to take chances. When it is making headway, a boat may rock." (Chinese Proverb).

Now is the time for courage. If not now, when? Today you have been presented with a unique opportunity. This is no time for hesitation, indecision or uncertainty. Act Now!! Be brave as you write goals, formulate intent and affirm commitment.

Visualize possibilities and promise in all that happens. Frame reality and events with love and optimism. As you do so the PDP will develop direction in your life. There are no mistakes, only learning and discovery. You are in control, you are the engineer. Trust your instincts especially when discarding the good or bad opinion of others in your formulations. You must choose independently if you are to grow.

The Personal Development Program will assuage all doubt. As your plan is implemented and intent asserted, you are set on a path. Progress is then evaluated and as the effectiveness of decisions is assessed, you will pursue alternatives more objectively. There is less room for reluctance and equivocation and more latitude for action and replanning. This results in greater certainty about your pursuits, thus setting up a cycle of determination and expectation. Anticipate success.

Fear of failure or discomfort is the great impediment to any type of growth and risk. Fear is frequently based on the projection of the bad opinions of others. When in such a frame of mind, we no longer listen to ourselves. Instead we imagine the reaction of others. Here we are wrong on two fronts, the first being reliance on outside approval for our behavior and self-worth. The second is that we can never know what another is thinking and all assumptions are simple projections of our own fears.

To conform to others' expectations is to chain yourself to the status quo. It is to find reasons for self-destructive behavior, and to stall when you want to move on. You've already been taking the easy way out by resisting action, which is why you now want change. Accept the challenge, move forward. There are no mistakes. You are either on the right path or on an alternative route which will ultimately lead you in the same direction, if only you look for the signs and persevere.

C. <u>Act now</u>

Fear of choosing is frequently based on defending a self-image which is both fragile and fraudulent. If you accept yourself and your faults as different aspects of a perfect you, defensiveness will no longer be necessary. Choosing can now become a part of the journey and a part of self-fulfillment and self-creation. Realize that whatever the result of a choice, your attitude towards your new situation is more important than your initial decision. Moving on and learning is the key to succeeding. Accomplishment is a unique and serpentine path filled with frustration and bewilderment but the answer is always there if you search and persist.

D. <u>Finding the signal through the noise</u>

"'Why didn't you walk around the hole?' asked the Tin Woodman.

'I don't know enough,' replied the Scarecrow cheerfully.'"
<u>(The Wizard of Oz</u>, 1900).

The PDP hones in on our goal by promoting awareness of empowerment and competence. There is a brief moment, a veritable nanosecond, that exists from the time something captures our attention to the time we interpret and decide to act. If we can take advantage of that flash, that instant between past and future to stop time, to transform the dance, then we can re-form our fate and re-create our essence and perspective. It is in that moment when awareness and intent merge we begin to control our future.

Use the PDP to hear the signal. Use it to expand, extend and evolve. Evolution is not linear. It is multi-layered with each area reinforcing growth in another. Opposing this is the force of regression, the desire to return to the safety of the known, of the unchanging and the protected.

Regression is an all encompassing, diffuse retreat to a previously safe but stagnant sector of being. Your choices affect everyone you know and everyone you encounter. Even the smallest act can have immeasurable consequences on others. "To pick a rose is to move a star." Move boldly but gently. Our choices are always between separation or unity, fear or love, decline or growth.

E. Preparing for change

"I have always thought myself very big and terrible; yet such little things as flowers came near to killing me, and such small animals . as mice have saved my life. How strange it all is!"
(The Wizard of Oz, 1900).

"First say to yourself what you would be; and then do what you have to do." (Epictetus, 55-135 AD).

All change spawns yet another choice, another decision and another opportunity to progress as we are gradually redefined. Trust and acceptance are the key virtues in this process. Trust in the greater plan and the beneficence of the universe will reinforce perseverance. Acceptance of "playing the hand that you are dealt" because this is the hand you were meant to have will repel doubt. This is the situation from which you will progress, prosper and persist. The results are not as significant as how you frame and interpret them.

The PDP will prepare you so that change is not considered an obstacle, or disruption. Rather, as a participant/observer, you will regard new circumstances as facts, results and input from your most recent experiment. Life is like an experimental laboratory in which we constantly test what works and what doesn't. From this perspective there can be no failure. When events do not transpire as hoped or expected, it is not bad but just another experience and extension towards insight and understanding. Such knowledge will modify or reinforce your behavior and mental attitude as you reassess and readjust. Each day is an occasion to reappraise and recreate your life.

Often the "insurmountable" is simply the untried. We are afraid to do something poorly, and to endure the frustrations of ineptitude. However, if we eradicate the arrogance that we must do all things well and foster a healthy humility that rewards pursuit more than perfection, we will succeed, one small step at a time. But we must embrace a willingness to be coarse, clumsy and confused. We must shift our perspective so that we reward ourselves for our attempts rather than our attainments.

Our PDP will direct attention to the effort and process rather than some amorphous, exemplary outcome. "If you find a thing difficult, consider whether it would be possible for any person to do it. Because anything that is humanly possible, that falls within human capabilities, you too can accomplish." (Marcus Aurelius, 121-180 CE).

F. <u>Erasing the past</u>

"'What makes you a coward?' asked Dorothy, looking at the great beast in wonder, for he was as big as a small horse."
(The Wizard of Oz, 1900).

"Finish each day and be done with it. You have done what you could. Some blunders and absurdities no doubt crept in; forget them as soon as you can. Tomorrow is a new day; begin it well and serenely and with too high a spirit to be encumbered with your old nonsense." (Ralph Waldo Emerson, 1803-1882 CE).

Get rid of antiquated attitudes as though you were cleaning your long gone college dorm. Make room for the new, the fresh, the untried. Dare to write it down, face fear, risk success and risk failure. Resist victimization. When you find yourself saying negative things, stop immediately. There is no room for pessimism. Perseverance is the key and your PDP can give you the determination to proceed. Always do something, keeping your eye on the prize, alerting yourself to the signals of success and the precursors of progress. When we take risks and intend action, our entire body responds with life and motivation; blood flow increases, oxygen intake works in conjunction with adrenaline, and we are excited by possibility. The very act and intent of decisiveness generates a sequence of basic biological rhythms that unerringly propel us towards action.

Writing gives you the courage to act and to recognize progress. It attunes you to achievement and sets the process of success in motion. You begin to identify and articulate your resistant, destructive thoughts and soliloquies. You become enabled to develop more effective strategies as you verge toward victory.

Focus on the present. How do you feel, what are your options, what are your circumstances <u>now</u>? The present contains the past and will determine the future. Your task is to be in the moment, to understand that this is all you have and all you need. All potential is in the day, the instant, the now, just waiting to be seized and realized.

As you re-read and reformulate your short-term PDP, you will discover your course. You will realize how seemingly random events come together and are consequential, thereby reinforcing motivation and reaffirming resolution. You will discover patterns and consequences where chaos and confusion once dwelled. Karl Jung (1875-1961) calls this "synchronicity." It is taking the events that occur together in space and time as "meaning something more than chance."

IV. Formulating a Plan

"First, have a definite, clear practical ideal, goal, or objective. Second, have the necessary means to achieve your goal--wisdom, money, materials, and methods. Third, adjust all your means to that goal. People are goal-seeking animals. Our lives only have meaning if we are reaching out and striving for our goals."
(Aristotle 384-322 BCE).

A. <u>Control</u>

*". . . if she could only get hold of the Silver Shoes they would give
her more power than all of the other things she had lost."*
<u>*(The Wizard of Oz,*</u> *1900).*

You have the power and the control to program the rest
of your life in this instant. However, you must supply the
motivation, intention, love, wisdom and courage. Each word
you write to establish goals and direction for the future erases
each word of your history that says "you can't." Your current
intent determines the future. The possibilities are limited only by
personal destructive discourse and self-constricted imagination.

All of your experience, both good and bad, if framed correctly
can amplify the moment. What you have achieved and what
you have not achieved make you exactly who you are, here and
now. What is happening at this second, writing the PDP and all
that preceded it was no accident, it was meant to happen. Get
to work! You'll never have a better chance to try your best and
become who you were meant to be.

B. <u>Long-term goals</u>

This is the heart of the Personal Development Program. It is
here where you both create and attest to the person you want to be
each day with each association. Past scholars have recommended
the cultivation of humility, gratitude, acceptance/forgiveness
and patience/trust. Read again the chapters on these ideals and
determine how they can be assimilated into routine behavior.

Consider the following questions before putting pen to paper
in the first draft of your agenda:

1. Who are you? Define yourself, e.g. the
    various roles of parent, child, spouse,
    coworker, friend, (casual or intimate/
    committed) etc.

2. Where do you see yourself right now?

3. What do you expect to accomplish in one year, five years?

4. What can you contribute to loved ones, associates and society in general?

5. Step outside yourself to be a participant/observer and describe your life as you would like it to be lived. Take your time!!

As you answer these questions and consider your responses, focus on six significant areas of functioning and potential:

1. Intellectual

2. Financial/Occupational

3. Social/Familial

4. Spiritual

5. Personal/Health (fitness and diet)

6. Emotional – ability to work, plan, love, and play

By becoming aware of these levels of external and internal engagement you clarify your purpose and define yourself. As such, you alter your perspective and consequently the ramifications of any situation. By means of this process, you become empowered and responsible. You are now ready to begin (see Appendix A for an example of a personal PDP).

C. <u>Avoiding fear</u>

"'And I should have been a coward for ever', declared the Lion, 'and no beast in all the forest would have had a good word to say to me.'" (<u>The Wizard of Oz</u>, 1900).

This process is not as scary as it sounds. Understand that the PDP, like the Constitution, is a malleable document, subject to amendments. The long-term goals of the PDP should be far less flexible than the short-term goals because they are expressions of the ideal self. This is your self-proclamation, your reference point and meaning. It should only be altered if the ideal is so unattainable that you begin to demean your attempts at achievement.

Short-term goals should be reviewed periodically, perhaps once a month. They should be refined and renovated as needed. So fear not. Failure will only happen if you do nothing. Sit, write and act. You are now in control and you will receive feedback from all attempts at change. This is information to use, not criticism to defend against. How you frame and label these results is significant. If you maintain a positive, objective perspective, you will move forward and grow.

The PDP itself reduces fear as you proceed. Writing enables you to clarify and control thoughts, ideas and emotions. You will begin to feel in command as concerns are addressed on paper and you construct a course of action to achieve goals. Intent will become more relevant and ambitions more attainable as you write. Your life will become like clay molded by purpose and fortified by awareness. You are now dictating your future being. The past brought you to this place so there are no regrets. You have learned and you are ready to start over, once again with a formative blueprint. As Lisa Nichols writes in <u>The Secret</u> (2006): "You were born to add something, to add value to this world. To simply be something, bigger and better than you were yesterday." Whatever mistakes we made, were through ignorance. We would have done better if we knew more. Now that we know what to do our only impediment is passivity.

D. Short-term goals

"Life is a series of collisions with the future; it is not the sum of what we have been, but what we yearn to be."
(Jose Ortega, 1883-1955).

This is where we activate. This is where the action is. Short-term goals should be structured and specific. They should be something we can do relatively easily each day. The main question is: what can I do today in small steps to achieve my long-term goals and to reinforce my PDP? "Success" is not an abstract concept just out of your reach. It is real, it is now. It is simply a matter of setting a goal and then acting on your intent. Just do it! Know yourself and make each small step achievable. Focus on fulfilling that task and "success" will follow. As we construct short-term goals, a plan of action emerges. Each encounter with others, each event and each challenge gives us the occasion to chip away at obstructions in order to engineer a new being whose power is untested yet all encompassing and boundless.

E. A general example

"It was easy to make the Scarecrow and the Lion and the Woodman happy, because they imagined I could do anything."
(The Wizard of Oz, 1900).

Utilizing daily deeds (in the form of short-term goals) to reinforce and objectify our more abstract ambitions is easier than it seems. For example, if a long-term goal is to show more gratitude to the people who have helped us and blessed our lives, a short-term goal may be to become more aware of their contributions and to promptly thank them each day. We may want to enter such events in a daily journal and each month write a note or make an extra effort to express gratitude. In this way we are able to measure progress in attaining long-term goals through realizing and implementing the simple, more specific, short-term goals.

271

By writing down and constructing activities with the intention of using them to accomplish the more complex and lofty ideals, we begin on the journey to advancement and maturation. Using a daily journal to keep focused, enhances the possibilities for success. However, such progress does not come easily. If it did we would have already achieved it. Understand and prepare for interruptions, obstructions and impediments. Be aware of demeaning self-talk and social pressure to remain static.

F. <u>Resisting resistance</u>

"A musician must make music, an artist must paint, a poet must write. If we are to be at peace with ourselves, we must be what we can be." (Abraham Maslow, 1908-1970).

The best advice for conquering any form of resistance is the Nike promo: "Just do it." Write it down and do it. Begin simply by sitting at a specified spot with pen and pad and write. Don't let self-censorship stifle you; this is your first draft so let it be filled with random notes and tangential thoughts. Write down what is happening now. If nothing else comes to you, write down that you're having trouble writing. What are your needs, thoughts and feelings at this moment, as you sit on this chair? Be bold and be you. You are perfectly you and you have a mission. Be proud, direct and sincere.

G. <u>Specific suggestions</u>

"The greatest mistake you can make in life is to be continually fearing you will make one." (Elbert Hubbard, 1856-1915).

1. Don't cross out and be honest. If you begin to think: "Should I write this?" you are probably on the right track to truth.

2. Writing takes on its own form and forces you in a direction of focus and clarity. Writing

272

will construct a method and means to achieve your goals. Therefore, just keep writing.

3. Write in the first person, e.g., "I am," "I want," "I will." In so doing you are being both introspective and reflective.

4. Be as specific as possible. This may be the most frustrating aspect of composing the PDP because it will force you to articulate and quantify goals that previously were vague and indeterminate.

5. Persist and persevere.

6. Persevere and persist.

7. Allow contradictions in your first draft. You can revisit and reconsider them at a later date.

8. Go from goal or effect (the general) to specific steps in increasingly difficult but tangible gradations so that you can monitor progress as you move ever closer to completion.

V. Summary

"As for the Scarecrow, having no brains, he walked straight ahead, and so stepped into holes and fell at full length on the hard bricks." (The Wizard of Oz, 1900).

"The secret of success is constancy to purpose." (Benjamin Disraeli, 1804-1881).

It is crucial to remember that both you and your Personal Development Program are works in progress. As you advance, you will either meet expectations or you will not. In the latter case you will learn and grow. In the current parlance this is a "win-win" situation. Persevere and you will succeed although it might not be in a way you expected. Through this process you will uncover your truth. You will quickly determine whether your expectations are unrealistic and unattainable. If this is the case, you simply re-evaluate, re-assess and re-plan. Cultivate the attitudes advocated here and your life will improve dramatically.

There was a reason you read this book and the opportunity is now to use it to your advantage. There are no chance occurrences, only beacons lighting the way. Your role is to believe, see and act.

As a final word, the prayer of St. Francis of Assisi (1181-1226) is presented as the paramount example of a long-term PDP. May all readers aspire to this:

"Lord,
make me an instrument of your peace.
Where there is hatred let me sow love;
Where there is injury, pardon;
Where there is doubt, faith;
Where there is despair, hope;
Where there is darkness, light; and
Where there is sadness, joy.
O divine Master,
grant that I may not so much
Seek to be consoled as to console;
To be understood as to understand;
To be loved as to love;
For it is in giving that we receive;
It is in pardoning that we are pardoned; and
It is in dying that we are born to eternal life."

VI. For Further Consideration

"Few things are impossible to diligence and skill. Great works are performed not by strength but by perseverance."
(Samuel Johnson, 1709-1784).

1. The purpose of the Personal Development Program is to help focus on goals and to commit to a course of action that can be accomplished.

2. The PDP is composed of long-term, more permanent goals and short-term, more immediate and flexible goals.

3. The ultimate purpose is to create a plan for advancement and self-evaluation that includes the development of humility, acceptance, gratitude, patience and courage leading to a life ruled by wisdom and love.

4. With a PDP you recreate your life and more effectively navigate change.

5. The PDP will help cultivate focus, intent and awareness which will become evident in everyday interactions, observations and assessments.

6. The PDP is a means to gain insight into emotions and to resolve past conflicts.

7. It is the responsibility of each individual and each individual alone to change and grow. We create our reality through framing, awareness and intent.

8. The PDP is our guide and support during times of turbulence and turmoil. It is our personal bible.

9. The PDP is essential if we are to shed the past, conquer dependency and progress towards empowerment, freedom and self-discovery.

10. The PDP helps face fear and challenge change.

11. The PDP increases the period between impulse and action.

12. All potential is in the moment. At all times, you are surrounded by everything you need to succeed.

13. As you re-read and reformulate the short-term PDP, you will clarify goals and appreciate how apparently random events come together and are consequential to the future.

14. You have the power and control to program the rest of your life, now.

15. Every experience, feeling and thought, whether good or bad, have prepared you for this moment.

16. Your purpose in life is unique and so is the PDP.

17. Throughout your life you can seize the moment and realize your dreams.

Good luck and God speed!

Namaste!

Appendix A

A Personal Development Program

I. Long-term intentions

A. Humility

I will continue to develop and refine the quality of humility. I will repel the natural tendency towards pride and arrogance in order to achieve greater acceptance of who I am and my unique mission in life. With humility, I will strive to serve others and come to understand that I am neither better nor worse. Rather, we are all united in a goal to make the world a more compassionate place. To this end, I will teach and learn, give and receive, forgive and accept.

B. Gratitude

I will cultivate the gift of gratitude in order to enhance my appreciation for all the blessings and persons enriching my life. I will consider these benefits as instruments to facilitate my journey to maturation. I understand that I am surrounded by everything I need and I will continue to be grateful as I acknowledge each day as a miracle.

C. Trust/Patience

I will trust in the beneficence of the universe and in the path that my higher power has placed before me. I understand that the great majority of events is beyond my control. Life will proceed on its own path, and at its own pace regardless of my wishes, hopes or actions. I will utilize what I am given for the benefit of all.

D. Acceptance/Forgiveness

I will accept the people and circumstances that enter my life with gratitude and humility. I will regard them as opportunities to help me learn and mature.

Similarly, I will forgive as I wish to be forgiven. I will recognize that I cannot control the behavior of others and that they too have a path to follow and a mission to accomplish. Rather than judging and comparing, I will regard all people with love and equanimity. I will avoid viewing their behavior as purposefully hurtful or aggressive.

I plan to cultivate these characteristics in all major areas of my life especially work, health, spirituality, social relations, finances, and intellectual growth.

II. Short-Term, Specific Goals

A. Humility

In order to focus on humility and increase my awareness and intent as a daily activity, I will intentionally seek opportunities to serve and expand kindness each day. I will carry out random acts of kindness and seek to assist others without being intrusive. I will provide emotional support through compliments and encouragement. Most importantly, I will not dissuade, deride or diminish the loving journey of another. Each day I will make a brief entry in my journal regarding these efforts.

B. Gratitude

I will expand awareness of life's blessings and benevolence by noting relevant observations in my journal each night. I will express gratitude more frequently. Thanking God and others will become routine. A prayer of gratitude will be offered each morning and evening to frame the day and sharpen awareness of my good fortune.

C. Trust/Patience

When confronted with challenges and the unexpected, I will reaffirm my trust in God and reassess what I can realistically accomplish and what must be surrendered. I will then concentrate my efforts on the achievable and not allow a desire for perfection to diminish the good. I will attest to the conviction that events are not defined by my needs and any setback is an opportunity to learn and mature. I will include a brief summary of such occurrences in my daily journal.

D. Acceptance/Forgiveness

Each day I will make a concerted effort to avoid being offended by someone's behavior. I will accept them and neither judge nor harbor resentment. When angry, destructive thoughts and feelings persist, I will pray until such animosity passes. I will persevere in my belief that whatever transpires in life is for a beneficial purpose and I will make every effort to react to all circumstances with humility, gratitude, patience and acceptance.

III. Daily Reminders

  A. Health—each day I will focus on eating
       nutritious food and exercising.

  B. Spiritual—each day will be dedicated to the
       service of God.

  C. Social—I will not try to change or control

others. I will be supportive and non-judgmental.

D. Financial–I will distinguish needs from wants, spend prudently and invest for my family's future.

E. Career–I will orient my responsibilities at work to the greatest service towards others.

F. Intellect–I will work consistently to learn new skills and new perspectives, so that I will be more effective in my life's work, and more compassionate in my social relations.

Appendix B

Thirteen Core Principles

1. Our life has meaning. We were born at a specific time, in a particular place, with a unique body, for a significant purpose.

2. All living things are part of a benevolent, grand design and as such deserve our respect, compassion and assistance.

3. We have little control over any external events or individuals but we can restrain responses by mastering our thoughts, feelings and behavior each moment with every interaction. We can therefore establish a loving, affirming reality.

4. We must resist self-destructive and self-denigrating thoughts in order to become who we were created to be.

5. The foundation for all positive personality traits is humility.

6. Of the four basic temperaments, acceptance/forgiveness is most related to contentment.

7. The gift of gratitude will either prevent or mitigate depression.

8. Patience/trust will allay anxiety.

9. Relationships are spiritual classrooms which present both challenges and opportunities for growth and self-knowledge.

10. Judgment and comparison are the most insidious qualities spawned by a consumer culture. They will destroy compassion, love, acceptance and unity.

11. Love and wisdom are composed of the same traits, namely humility, gratitude, acceptance/forgiveness, and patience/trust.

12. Love is the emotional expression of wisdom and wisdom is the intellectual expression of love.

13. Courage combines all these traits and motivates us to interact with others, confront change and express wisdom and love.

Bibliography

And Suggested Reading

Albom, Mitch. Tuesdays with Morrie. New York: Anchor Books, 1997.

Baum, L. Frank. The Wizard of Oz. London: Puffin Books, 1994.

Boorstein, Sylvia. Pay Attention for Goodness' Sake. New York: Ballantine Books, 2002.

Bowlby, John. Attachment and Love. London: Hogarth Press, 1969.

Buddhist Society (Ed.). 1001 Pearls of Buddhist Wisdom. London: Duncan Baird Publishers, 2006.

Byrne, Rhonda. The Secret. New York: Atria Books, 2006.

Casey, Karen. Daily Meditations for Practicing the Course. San Francisco: Hazelden Foundation, 1995.

Chantrell, Glynnis (Ed.). The Oxford Dictionary of Word Histories. Oxford: Oxford University Press, 2002.

Chopra, Deepak. The Path to Love. New York: Three Rivers Press, 1997.

Chopra, Deepak. The Book of Secrets. New York: Harmony Books, 2004.

Covey, Stephen R. The 7 Habits of Highly Effective People. New York: Simon & Schuster, 1989.

Das, Lama Surya. The Big Questions. United States of America: Holtzbrinck Publishers, 2007.

Das, Lama Surya. Buddha Is as Buddha Does. San Francisco: Harper, 2007.

Dyer, Wayne W. Your Sacred Self. New York: Harper Paperbacks, 1995.

Dyer, Wayne W. <u>Wisdom of the Ages</u>. New York: Harper Collins Publishers, 1998.

Dyer, Wayne W. <u>Manifest Your Destiny</u>. New York: Harper Paperbacks, 1999.

Dyer, Wayne W. <u>There's a Spiritual Solution to Every Problem</u>. New York: Harper Collins Publishers, 2004.

Dyer, Wayne W. <u>You'll See It When You Believe It</u>. New York: Quill, 2001.

Foundation for Inner Peace. <u>A Course in Miracles</u>. Tiburon. CA: Foundation for Inner Peace, 1976.

Fromm, Erich. <u>Escape from Freedom</u>. New York: Holt, Rinehart & Winston, 1941.

Hazelden Foundation. <u>Keep It Simple</u>. San Francisco: Hazelden Foundation, 1989.

Jung, Carl G. <u>Analytical Psychology</u>. New York: Moffat, Yard, 1916.

Jung, Carl G. <u>Modern Man in Search of a Soul</u>. New York: Harcourt, Brace & World, 1933.

Karen, Robert, Ph.D. <u>The Forgiving Self</u>. New York: Doubleday, 2001.

Klauser, Henriette Anne. <u>Write It Down, Make It Happen</u>. New York: Simon & Schuster, 2000.

Ladner, Lorne. <u>The Lost Art of Compassion</u>. New York: Harper Collins Publishers, 2004.

Lama, Dalai and Cutler, Howard C. <u>The Art of Happiness</u>. New York: Penguin Putnam Inc., 1998.

Oliver, Joan Duncan. <u>Good Karma</u>. London: Duncan Baird Publishers, 2006.

Rainer, Tristine. <u>The New Diary</u>. New York: Penguin Putnam, Inc., 1978.

Ray, Veronica. <u>Choosing Happiness: The Art of Living Unconditionally</u>. Hazelden Foundation. San Francisco: Harper, 1991.

Rogers, Carl R. <u>On Becoming a Person</u>. Boston: Houghton Mifflin, 1961.

Ross, David. 1001 Pearls of Wisdom. London: Duncan Baird Publishers, 2006.

Ruiz, Don Miguel. The Voice of Knowledge. San Rafael, CA: Amber-Allen Publishing, 2004.

Ryan, M. J. Attitudes of Gratitude. Boston: Conari Press, 1999.

Ryan, M. J. The Power of Patience. New York: Broadway Books/Random House, 2003.

Ryan, M. J. Trusting Yourself. New York: Broadway Books, 2004.

Ryan, M. J. The Happiness Makeover. New York: Broadway Books, 2005.

Tolle, Eckhart. The Power of Now. Novato, CA: New World Library, 1999.

Wiener, Philip P. (Ed.). Dictionary of the History of Ideas (Vol. III). New York: Charles Scribner's Sons, 1973.

Williamson, Marianne. A Return to Love. New York: Harper Collins Publishers, 1992.

Williamson, Marianne. Everyday Grace. New York: Riverhead Books, 2002.

Williamson, Marianne. A Gift of Change. New York: Harper Collins Publishers, 2004.

Williamson, Marianne. The Age of Miracles. Carlsbad, CA: Hay House, 2008.

Wolf, Fred Alan. Dr. Quantum's Little Book of Big Ideas. Needham, MA: Moment Point Press, 2005.

Zukav, Gary. The Seat of the Soul. New York: Simon & Schuster, 1999.